Secret Guide To Wives For Husbands

To Strengthen Your Marriage Or Fix It

I know you're not married but it's about how women think. What guy isn't curious about that?! I wish you had been my mom's husband.

By Norman Anayeland

You'll always be dad.
Love, Shadow

Secret Guide to Wives For Husbands
To Strengthen Your Marriage Or Fix It

Relationships, Self-Improvement, Self-Awareness, Personal Growth, Marriage

Books may be purchased by contacting
the publisher at: www.secret-guide.com

Library of Congress Control Number: 2020906469
ISBN: 978-1-952649-00-4 (paperback)
ISBN: 978-1-952649-01-1 (ebook)

First Edition, 2020

Disclaimer: This publication is sold with the understanding that the author is not engaged in rendering psychological, medical or other professional services. If expert assistance or counseling is needed, the services of a competent professional should be sought.

Published in Cranston, Rhode Island

10 9 8 7 6 5 4 3 2 1

Dedication

This book is dedicated, in loving memory, as promised
to
Frances V. Farrell and Francis E. Farrell

Table of Contents

Introduction

Welcome to the Secret Guide to Women for Married Men. Whether you're just considering buying this book or you've already bought it, we want to congratulate you! The first step to saving your marriage is to *do* something to save it. If you're searching for answers, you've taken the first, and possibly most important, step.

The Secret Recipe

Here's the whole secret and nothing but the secret:

If your wife feels you're attracted to her and love her, and she feels she's attracted to you and loves you, there will be no problems in your marriage.

Yup. That's it.

Of course, we're going to need the rest of the book to explain it.

The point is that what's in your heart it's not as important as how your spouse *feels* about what's in your heart. Her feelings aren't driven by your feelings. They're driven by how you express those feelings with your actions and words.

If you genuinely love your spouse but there are problems in your marriage, those problems are driven by the way you express that love. Of course, not all marital issues come from a lack of love. Many people divorce because they have disagreements over how they spend their leisure time, how they spend money, clashes in value systems, and so on. However, we believe that these issues stem from a lack of ability to communicate and resolve problems in a productive way. And this challenge results from a fundamental miscommunication about love.

If your wife feels you're attracted to and love her, and she feels the same, there's a willingness to resolve practical issues. When you were dating, you probably didn't have the problems you have right now. Something changed. Maybe a lot of things changed. But the underlying fundamental change can be traced back to the fact that when you were dating you both felt loved. That created a desire to listen to and accommodate the other person. Now that you've been married for some time, one or both parties is not as willing to give the other the benefit of the doubt and put aside their feelings in favor of whatever helps the relationship thrive. In short, because one or both parties doesn't feel "loved", they are more resistant to cooperation to resolve these issues.

When you're "in love" there's a sublimation of the ego, the part of a person that is most interested in its own opinion and feelings, to the relationship. The interest is much more in what is good for the couple as a unit. But that can only last so long. No one can put their own feelings on the back burner indefinitely. As the ego starts to assert itself, the interpretation is that you're no longer "in love." Because we've been raised to believe that the most important aspect of a relationship is being "in love", there's a tendency to question the relationship.

If you and your wife can bring back that feeling of being "in love", you can bring your relationship back to how it used to feel. In order to do that, you must be able to understand what she's communicating accurately and respond to that. You also must be able to communicate your love to her in a way she can understand and appreciate. This book will help you develop practical skills to understand what she's trying to communicate, how to address her concerns, and how to relate your feelings in a way she can understand.

I Understand, Therefore I Change

By the time you finish this book, you should have a decent grasp of what you need to do to make your wife feel that you are attracted to and love her. We will also try to give you a solid foundation in what you need to do to maximize the chance that she will be attracted to and love you.

If you are successful in properly using this book in the way it was intended, we have no doubt that your marriage will be free of problems.

Does that sound like a "disclaimer?" Good. It is. And that's the other thing we can promise you; in writing this guide, we have been uncompromisingly honest and relentlessly thorough.

Despite working as diligently as we could to start every concept from the most incontrovertible facts we could find, there will still be plenty of work for you to do. Maybe other books believe in *I Understand, Therefore I Change*. We disagree; all we know for sure is that *if you change, your marriage will change.*

Although we sincerely tried to break the topics into what we thought would be a manageable amount of information and to organize it in a way that would promote understanding, we recognize that the truth is every chapter is related to and interdependent on the others. As often as possible, we tried to make those connections for you, acknowledging (to ourselves) that we were arbitrarily presenting something as linear, (starting at one point, proceeding in a straight line and ending at some distance from the start,) when in fact it's anything but.

For example, if your wife's favorite phrase is, "Fine. Whatever." And it drives you bonkers. You will learn in "What Are You Really Saying?" what she's trying to communicate (the opposite of "fine"), how she's communicating it (metamessages), why she's using this method to communicate (underlying issues), how to identify other metamessages (they're out of place for the conversation or the situation), how to implement a short-term "fix" (move the topic from covert to overt), and how to implement a long-term "fix" (address the underlying problem). But to do that, you would need to improve the romance in your marriage (first two chapters), learn to more properly manage expectations (third chapter), build up trust (fourth chapter) and adjust the way you communicate with her (fifth through seventh chapters). To do this you will need to gain insight into how her past has helped bring you to your present, to gain the ability to paraphrase, to understand what actions need to take and how to execute them, to improve your problem solving skills and to learn how to address grudges should that fail (all of the remaining chapters.)

Yet, despite the interdependency, we have carefully arranged the topics to get them into "order," so we do want to caution you against skipping ahead at any time.

Target Audience – Who Should Read This Book?

Anyone can read this book and get something out of it. We're expecting that the types of men who will be attracted to this guide will be those who are married and have the feeling that their marriage isn't going exactly the way they would like it to go. We realize that this is a wide spectrum. Maybe it's not satisfying for you, whatever that may mean. Perhaps your spouse doesn't seem to be happy or isn't as engaged as she once was. It could just mean you aren't having as much sex as you would like. Or it could mean all hell is breaking loose, you fight like cats and dogs every night, and you have a sneaking suspicion that she may be thinking of leaving.

We'll be addressing all of those issues with practical information on how to discover *what's* wrong, what *went* wrong, and, most important, how to fix it.

While we believe the information in this book could be helpful for those who aren't yet in a long-term committed relationship, and it could be helpful for those who have been in a long-term committed relationship and are separated or in the process of a divorce, the target audience is for people who are beyond the making a commitment phase and are not in an active separation.

This guide is aimed at men, specifically for heterosexual (married) men. While there is a possibility it could be useful for men who want to improve or save their marriage to another man (and if it is, we'd love to hear that,) the book is tailored to addressing issues that arise in heterosexual marriages.

Anyone can take much of the information inside this guide and adapt it to other situations. But if you're not a man who is married to a woman, please don't feel offended that the text isn't going to make any real effort to address your situation. In future, we may have a publication that speaks to your concerns. If you are looking for that, please contact us at www.secret-guide.com and let us know.

Our goal in writing this guide is to create something that addresses what we feel is a deficit in this field. The authors of this book are a team of writers. They constitute both men and women, with backgrounds in multiple fields. As such, we have collectively read a lot of books on this topic in our own quests for knowledge and help. As a group, we found that as it regards self-help books aimed at improving relationships, we all had similar complaints:

1. Either not honest about or not specific enough in identifying the audience: the book claimed to be address helping couples equally but left the impression that it favored one side or the other.

2. Too much theory: the book was inundated with "examples" or scientific facts but failed to make the connection to how that information could be applied; at the end we understood *why* there was a breakdown in Bob and Mary's relationship but remained confused as to *how* that was supposed to relate to our marriage.

3. Not practical enough: the book explained *why* in a convincing way, but there just wasn't enough *how*. It seems like some authors think if they can provoke us into documenting *what* is going on, without telling us *how* to fix it, the problem will somehow resolve itself. Or, they explain the differences between men and women, create a structure that provides "guided" activities, and somehow this is supposed to translate into good communication. There always seems to be a "gap" between the text and life that we have to fill without understanding exactly what we are supposed to put there.

To that end, we've tried to create a guide for a very specific audience. We don't use any examples from couples we've counseled. If there are examples, they're hypothetical. We just made something up to illustrate the point. The techniques we're going to teach you can't just work for Bob and Mary, or just for anyone we would be counseling in person. This is a book. We don't get to have a dialogue with you. What we present must be compelling in written form; essentially as a broadcast with no opportunity for you to ask for additional information or clarification. To that end, we've tried to anticipate your reaction and address questions or concerns that we think you might logically have in the text as they arise.

We spent comparatively little time on inventing examples. This is because we're providing "rules" that we think would (and should) address *any* situation. We don't see any value in relating two to four examples of other people who might have had problems that sort of might be like the problems we think our readers might have. Everyone is unique with their own unique situations. Instead, we chose cheesy stereotypes (or artificially exaggerated behavior) that illustrate the *type* of situation the information applies to, and we expect you to extrapolate that to your own experience. To assist you in understanding the "rules," we've provided "take-aways" at the end of every chapter. It is not enough to just read the take-aways. They're a recap, not a replacement of the contents of the chapter.

Our focus is on providing you excellent customer service. For us, that means providing a superior product that maximizes your investment. Sure, it's nice to learn how men and women are different; it's interesting and thought provoking. But if our title attracted you, then you have problems to solve. You don't need a book that's going to waste your time with a lot of stories about someone else's problems and how *they* solved them. This probably isn't a research project for you. Most likely you need something you can use right away. When a relationship is less than ideal, every day seems like an eternity. We won't waste your time. What we ask in return is that you read carefully. The book is dense. If you don't take time to really understand the information, it won't be as effective.

Disclaimer

A significant portion of this book will analyze the differences between men and women. We will be working with stereotypes. Please understand, we realize not all men and women fit every stereotype. There are men who in some ways behave like women on certain topics and vice versa. There may be times during the day when people move fluidly between both styles.

We don't expect you to check your brain at the door. Read what we have to say, then evaluate your situation. If it doesn't exactly fit, is there anything helpful you can take from it? The point is not to perpetuate stereotypes. But they exist because something is often true for a majority of a group. We don't expect you to match exactly and we certainly don't want to limit anyone. But, let's face it, all "self-help" books are generic. The value comes from what you make of it. Please don't let yourself get caught up in minutia. Ask yourself, "What can I take from this that will be useful to me in my situation?" Then act accordingly.

The Plan – How To Read This Book

The mind isn't dramatically different than the stomach. We tend to gorge on foods we like. Few people ever leave a buffet so bloated on broccoli they can barely move. And even those broccoli lovers will admit that once you've eaten your fill, no matter how many wonderful things are on the table, you just have to give yourself some time to digest before you can chow down again.

We expect some of the things in this book will be "tastier" than others. We are not suggesting this is the definitive guide to your specific spouse. What we do suggest is that before you discard any portion of any chapter, give it some time to digest and think about it. You might want to share it with your spouse and get her opinion. If she agrees that the content has nothing to do with her, then hey! That's one more thing that you agree on. Just knowing you've purchased the book and are putting in the work to make your marriage better might work wonders in and of itself. But the chapters build on each other. Even if you don't feel something is applicable, please do make an effort to understand it before moving on or it will get to a point where it just doesn't make sense.

We also suggest you take some time on the chapters that you feel will be the most helpful to you. We're not going to say something silly like "read one and exactly one chapter a day" or tell you how you learn best. That would be dumb on our part; because, at a basic level, we don't know you. Maybe you want to read the book cover to cover, put it away for a day or two and then reread the chapters individually. Maybe you do need to read one chapter a day. Only you know the system that will work best for you. All we want to do is remind you that the brain, like the stomach, can only take in so much until it's saturated. For the information to be truly useful you're going to need to digest it mentally and implement changes. Reading this book won't change your marriage for better or for worse. Unless you *apply* this information to your specific situation, nothing is going to change.

We want you to achieve your goals. We worked hard on this book. Please give it the attention it deserves.

What This Book Can't Do

This isn't a legal disclaimer, but we feel we would be remiss if we didn't include something. If you've bought or you're interested in buying this book, chances are there is trouble in paradise. We can't guarantee you that if you implement every bit of advice we give, your relationship will be perfect at the end of it. We can't even promise you that you won't end up losing the relationship. It could be that your spouse has already decided to end the marriage, and there's nothing you can do to change her mind. We hope not, and sorry to be such a downer! But this isn't a magic wand and we're not guardian angels with a hotline to the spirit world.

The only thing we're promising is to give you the benefit of our insight into this topic. This book was produced by a team of writers who have a great deal of experience, both academic and personal. We could tell you that between the writers we have over one hundred fifty years of relationship experience. We could tell you that our team includes people who have studied with experts in the field. Certainly, we could list a string of degrees to impress you with how much money we've spent having academic institutions validate our research. Or maybe you would be more impressed if we said we have a combined experience of seven divorces (so we know what DOESN'T work) and about sixteen years of happy marriages. All of these facts are true. But are they a compelling reason to buy this book?

We don't think so. Individually, we've spent thousands of dollars on resources for building relationships. None of those factors made a difference to us when we made our purchases. Yeah, it might have said "Written by so and so who has done such and such for however long and is considered an expert on whatever." But once we opened the books and started reading, they either were giving helpful information, or they weren't. Sometimes we were glad to spend fifteen dollars on a book that had only one paragraph that made a difference at the exact right moment. As you can see, we've made no effort to try to win your trust by trotting out credentials to use to impress you. We hope every page brings you new insight, coping tools and closer to your goals. We also believe it doesn't matter who wrote the book if what they wrote rang true and helped you in your time of need.

Use your best judgement. At the risk of being hokey, listen to your heart. Pay the most attention to the things that feel right or ring true for you.

What matters is if what we wrote has meaning for you and is helpful.

We sincerely hope that is the case and send our best wishes and prayers with you on your journey.

And now, without further ado ....

Chapter One

Romance: Just A Box Of Chocolates?

"It's not you, it's me."

Let's Start At The End; A Very Good Place To Start

There's nothing more frustrating than the tried and true "It's not you, it's me." If it's any consolation, we don't buy it.

So, your marriage is less than ideal. Before we jump into how to fix it, we're going to spend just a little time exploring why relationships end. If you aren't interested, just skip to the next chapter and our feelings won't be hurt. But we think understanding *why* is a big part of understanding *how* to fix something. That's what makes the old saw, "It's not you, it's me" so cruel. On the surface, it might be meant to soften the blow on the person being dumped. Certainly. that's what you'll find on Wikipedia if you plug it into Google's search engine. We don't agree. What we think it really means is, "I'm not going to tell you *why* I'm leaving, either because I don't respect you enough to believe you can understand or because I am so determined to leave I don't want to give you any insight into my motive." And that's the optimistic interpretation. What that phrase really does is deny the person being dumped any possible sense of closure and certainly deprives them of any type of learning experience. At the extreme, it might be a cruel way of saying, "I'm so angry with you that I'm leaving, and I want to make sure my leaving haunts you and leaves you insecure for the rest of your life."

So why *do* relationships end?

At a basic level, they end because one or both parties are no longer getting their needs met by being in the relationship.

We could give you a song and dance about love fading, and that might be true, but we're hoping to leave you in a better place than we found you. We feel confident that this explanation gets to the heart of the problem.

If your relationship is in jeopardy, and you're not the disgruntled party, (or even if you are), then you probably are driving yourself crazy wondering, *why?* When we ask ourselves, "What went wrong?" What we really mean is, "Why is this happening?" If you're going to play detective, then remember one of the main things detectives look for is a motive.

Humans don't generally do things for no reason. Not discounting altruistic behavior like volunteering for charities and so on, let's agree that human behavior is purposeful and self-centered.

If that offends you, then we apologize. But we think if you take a moment to think about it, you will probably agree. What drew you to your spouse to begin with? Most likely you liked the way being with that person made you feel. Why did you commit to a relationship with that person? Because you didn't want to *not be* with that person.

What causes that to end? Well, if entering a relationship is driven by the need for the feelings that you get when you're with that person, then it stands to reason that the relationship will end when you no longer feel that way.

Of course, we're oversimplifying. Plenty of people get into relationships and marriage for lots of reasons besides "it's fun" and "I like spending time with that person" – or do they? If you got married because you were expecting a child out of wedlock or because your parents arranged it or whatever reason you might be thinking of listing, is that really different than saying "I got married because I expected my experience of life to be better if I were married than if I were not"?

So, if marriage, or any kind of long-term commitment, is driven by needs gratification, then it stands to reason that the end of the commitment is driven by a lack of needs gratification.

Of course, we could have spent this whole book on this topic. Don't worry, we're not going to do that. But it is worth thinking about this: according to Sir Isaac Newton, a body in motion will stay in motion. That's a pretty scientific way of saying *things change for a reason.* If your spouse "loved" you enough to commit, then it's unlikely that they just suddenly woke up one morning thinking, "Well, that was nice. but I think I'm done." It's not easy for anyone to end a relationship, even if it feels that way. While we could argue that some people just struggle with commitment or others are just born cheaters, if that were the only explanation then there would be no point in writing about it.

So while we acknowledge that there might be relationships that were "doomed to end" because of fatal character flaws, we're writing from the standpoint that the end of the relationship was caused because it ceased to meet the needs of one or both of the participants.

Why would that be the case? Well, again, thinking logically, either the behavior of one of the parties changed or the needs of one of the parties changed. Those are the two things that could happen to change the equation.

Only you know which one applies to your relationship.

We think it's common that behavior changes over time. When you first meet someone, it's new and exciting. Have to work late? No problem! You still magically have the energy to stay up talking until three in the morning learning about each other. After ten years of marriage, two kids and four dogs, is that still going to be the case? Probably not. But that's a change.

It's human nature to be on your best behavior when you're in a new situation. Whenever you chose to move in with your spouse or future-spouse, you were probably at your best during that time. Now, most likely your behavior has changed.

We're not going to let her off the hook either. It's very possible and very likely her behavior has changed as well. Even if you don't have kids or pets, just being together for a long time can generate changes in behavior. When you add into that the changes that accompany age, a new job, different house, economics – well, you get the idea. So, what is different about your or her behavior as compared to when you met?

The other problem is changing expectations. The stereotype is that women get married hoping they can change the man; men get married hoping the woman won't change. Even without that, people's needs may change over time. This could be for several reasons. Needs change based on internal desires and external forces. Maybe it was acceptable to live in a messy house in your twenties but in your thirties that's not what you want. Maybe when you first got married you needed your spouse to work and now, because you got a promotion, you don't. Change doesn't have to be negative.

One of the things that might cause what appears to be a "need change" is a failure to have strong communication before the marriage. Unfortunately, not everyone communicates clearly and honestly with their spouse. If one or both partners enter a marriage with secret goals or hopes which they have not communicated to the other, when it becomes clear that those goals or hopes are not being met, they become disenchanted. That person is no longer "meeting their needs" even though they never met them before. Part of the need that used to be met was the expectation of need satisfaction in the future; kind of an IOU for a need that is called in at some arbitrary point in the marriage, usually without warning.

Romancing A Stone

That brings us to the concept of romance.

Most couples define romance as, "Non-essential behavior that communicates love through extra-ordinary acts." And it's one of the first things that dies in a relationship that's struggling. Once the extra rush of hormones from a new relationship ends and the reality of life with its financial stresses, lack of time, and emotional burdens sets in, making that extra effort we call romance gets harder and harder. It becomes easier to think, "Well, we're married. (S)he knows how I feel. What's the big deal?"

It is a big deal.

In fact, it's the whole deal.

But it's hard to understand using if the definition above is your definition.

As far as we're concerned, romance should be defined as, "all behavior that communicates love every day." Period.

We can't talk about the specific needs that being in a relationship met for your individual spouse. But we believe that the vast majority of women get into relationships and then commit to those relationships because of romance. And by romance, we don't just mean a box of chocolates or flowers, whether for a specific reason or no reason.

When a relationship is new, there is inherently a need to get to know the other person. In order to facilitate this exchange of information the two parties give each other a lot of attention. Even when you weren't buying flowers and chocolates, you were probably chatting each other up until three am and hanging on each other's words.

As time goes on, you don't have that strong a need to exchange information because, at a practical level, you've learned it. If you don't replace that early attention with some other form of attention as the relationship matures, you will lose the romance.

Romance = Attention

Most of the media to which men are exposed teach the lesson that romance is made up of grand, and often expensive, gestures that couldn't possibly be made very frequently. If "Diamonds are a girl's best friends"[1] then what happens to the guy who's poor? If you needed a greeting card every time you wanted your spouse to know how you feel, then your greeting card budget would be greater than even the biggest coffee snob's latte budget. If you want to know about romance, read a romance book or watch a "chick flick." Sure, there may be some grand gestures, but the average romance heroine is wooed by a series of unspectacular events. Putting aside the "love at first sight" attraction, what gets them every time is the amount of attention the hero gives the heroine.

While one shouldn't disqualify the quality of the attention, and much of the rest of this book will be dedicated to the quality, the quantity is just as, if not more, important. Again, we can't speak about your spouse, but most women will give you almost as many points for trying as for succeeding.

Romance is not a temporary state of action. It's a permanent state of being. You might think its unrealistic to expect that intense attention that exists during the "honeymoon" phase of the relationship, whether that's a few weeks or a few years, to last forever. We think it's more unrealistic to expect someone

---

1 https://en.wikipedia.org/wiki/Diamonds_Are_a_Girl%27s_Best_Friend

who fell in love with a person behaving in a certain way not to feel less than enthusiastic when that behavior changes. That's *why* when a woman accuses a man of a negative behavior people say, "Oh, oh, the honeymoon is over." That phrase means "she's discovered how you behave when the relationship isn't new and you're on your best behavior." Whether it's the behavior of the man or the woman, isn't it a kind of bait and switch if you behave one way during courtship and totally differently thereafter? If you bought a car that got a certain miles per gallon during the test drive and then was totally different after you bought it, wouldn't you complain?

That is also not to say that you or anyone will give their spouse the exact same attention you gave when you first met. It is true that now you have the information you probably don't need to exchange that information all the time. But the good news is that you can turn everyday acts into acts of romance. How you greet your spouse in the morning; how you negotiate what to have for dinner; how you decide what to watch on television can all be expressions of romance.

The fact of the matter is that most likely when you first met and throughout the "good" period of your marriage, almost everything you did was romantic because it showered your spouse with attention and conveyed your love. Unless her needs have changed, if you return to this behavior, it should revitalize your marriage.

Some readers might be thinking, "Are you saying my wife is a spoiled brat who needs me to pay attention to her every minute of every day?"

Not at all.

Women are "ranked" in society by their ability to take care of others. If her husband and children, or anyone else who is her responsibility is successful, that will be a feather in her cap as a caregiver. What a woman looks for in a spouse is someone who cares about her. Love, then, is when she feels she's the most important person in her husband's life. The only way she would know that this is true is by the amount of attention that he shows her. If his focus is on her, then he loves her. If his focus is not on her, then he doesn't love her.

We're not saying that your spouse can't feel your love when you're not paying attention to her. But women are much less likely to interpret something you do for them in absentia as love than something you do for them directly. For example, you might feel like going to work every day is an act of love that you do for your wife. That may be true. But it's unlikely your wife will interpret you going to work as an act of love. It's more likely that if you spend too much time at work, she'll interpret that as something you're doing to forward your career or meet one of your own goals, rather than something you're doing specifically for her.

If your spouse's needs have changed, you will need to put in some extra effort to find out what her needs are now and establish a plan of action to make sure you're meeting them. But as you progress through the rest of the book, we will try to be as concrete as possible, giving you practical rules you can follow.

The take-aways from this chapter are:

1. Relationships thrive on romance.

2. Romance = Attention

3. Romance isn't a special occasion; it's an everyday state of being.

Chapter Two

Prince Charming Or The Frog?

To summarize the story of the Frog Prince, a spoiled princess loses an item in a pond, and it's retrieved by a talking frog in exchange for a promise of friendship. After the princess becomes enamored with the frog and kisses him, he turns into a handsome prince. So, to some extent, our title is a little misleading. It's not Prince Charming *or* the frog; the frog *is* Prince Charming.

But we think that's an important point. Whether it's the Frog Prince or Beauty and the Beast, we've all been raised on the idea that someone who might initially be unattractive for some reason hides the perfect lover who is only revealed by an act of faith when it comes to love. Conversely, there are plenty of examples where someone of physical beauty is a less than ideal partner due to their personality.

While this concept is often targeted at men, there are plenty of examples in pop culture for women as well. The good news is (hopefully) no one is looking for the perfect spouse. There's some tolerance for physical deviation. What we're interested in is *why* in all these stories the "frog" or "beast" turns into a prince and what that means for men in the context of their relationships.

Aside from the obvious problems of procreating with another species, there are two main points we can take from these metaphors.

Turn And Face The Change

First, the idea that if you just love someone enough, they will change or morph into the ideal person. This is a critical concept for a man to understand in his relationship with a woman. Women are taught to be the WD40 of the relationship; they smooth things over. They're masters of deferred gratification. Women are, generally, taught not to assert their needs. Instead, they sublimate them to the needs of the relationship or the family.

It's important to know *deferred* does not mean *dismissed*. When someone doesn't get what they want the need doesn't go away just because they give in. It's a very typical experience for men that in an argument a woman brings up things that have happened in the past which the man thought was settled. That's because when men negotiate, they don't give in until they achieve a compromise with which they can live. (Obviously we're majorly generalizing; we understand that this is not *all* men and not *all* compromises.) Women, however, are taught from a young age that it's better to give in to keep the peace than to hold out for what they really want. Unfortunately, they're also taught that if they just give enough, eventually they will get everything they want. If the frog gets enough kisses, he will become the prince. Unfortunately, every woman has a different (secret) idea of what "enough" actually means.

The practical ramifications of this is that you can "win" an argument that is actually a "loss." Further, these smalls "wins" can create the equivalent of a ticking relationship time bomb that can explode at any time.

What can you do about this? Plenty of things. Make sure you pay extra attention to the metamessages chapters later in this book which will provide further detail on this phenomenon and practical advice on how to deal with it. For this chapter, you need to be aware that your spouse may have entered the relationship with hidden expectations. There may be aspects of your personality or behavior that she considers to be a "frog" that she's been working to change into a "prince."

We realize some of the men reading this may think, "Well, she married me. I'm not going to change who I am to suit who she thinks I should be." We understand and support your feelings. But, if any of those things are "deal breakers", then you're going to have to decide what is more important: this behavior or the marriage? We also feel that if you're in this situation, even if she considers the behavior to be a "deal breaker" it doesn't necessarily mean that you have to change.

First, you're going to need to find out if in fact there are any behaviors that your spouse considers undesirable. Whether you agree or not, when someone is annoyed with someone else's behavior, that behavior becomes disproportionately important. Think of it like this. A drop of water dripping off a ledge falling onto a rock doesn't mean much. But if that dripping continues for years it can wear a hole right through the toughest substance. The sum of the effect is much greater than any individual drop of water. In this way, small behaviors that grate on her nerves can eventually destroy the entire relationship.

There are two ways you can discover hidden problems. First, start paying attention to small feedback that reoccurs on a regular basis. With a man you can generally gauge his emotional investment in a topic based on the amount of emotion he conveys when talking about that topic. If a man is yelling about something, it's a pretty good guess that he's passionate about that topic. If he just makes an offhand comment on a subject, it's unlikely he feels strongly about it. Because they are taught to avoid creating conflict, women do not always convey the degree to which they feel passion when discussing a topic. Expressing a strong opinion almost always creates conflict.

You might be lucky and be married to a spouse who was raised to express her feelings clearly and completely. But if you're not, you will have to do some detective work. Many men say, "It's like she wants me to read her mind" but we don't think that's true. It's more accurate to say, "She wants me to pay attention to small clues that add up to big information." Maybe every time you leave your socks on the floor, she makes a comment or a joke about this habit when she picks them up. Be particularly attentive to subjects about which she uses sarcasm. Sarcasm is, "the use of irony to mock or show contempt." Any subject about which she's sarcastic means she's showing contempt for that behavior. Those small, frequent expressions of contempt signal emotion that can build up over time to create an explosion.

The second way you can discover these hidden problems is by asking her. If she makes a comment about leaving socks on the floor that's a great opportunity to say something simple like, "Does that really bother you, honey?" Some women, particularly if you've been in a relationship for a while, might be reluctant to confess their real feelings. That might seem strange to a man. If you have feelings, why not articulate them? Unfortunately, you're again fighting society's programming here. The princess simply kisses the Frog; she doesn't give the command "Turn into a prince!" and then bestow the kiss. Women are often taught that there is something wrong with asking for what you want or offering criticism. You may have to ask a couple of times or reassure her that it's safe to just tell you how she feels.

Other men reading this may be thinking, "Reluctance to offer criticism? Not my wife!" We understand that not all women are reluctant to offer criticism, and in fact, many women seem to be fond of "nagging." If your spouse is a "nag", you need to pay attention to that. While you might feel that the topics of "nagging" are unimportant, they're clearly important to her. That doesn't mean you must do everything she wants you to do, when she wants you to do it. What it does mean is you have to do a better job of communicating and setting expectations.

Leader Of The Pack

The second main point we can learn from the parable of the Frog Prince, is that women are social creatures. It's important for men to remember this fact.

If the princess is in love with the frog, then why does he need to turn into a prince? Again, let's take out the obvious difficulty of procreating with a frog. Even if the princess is satisfied with her relationship with the frog, it's unlikely the king would approve of his daughter marrying beneath her. Unlikely the queen would be excited, not to mention all the subjects of the realm. Because relationships are social constructs, the frog *must* turn into a prince. Right or wrong, society will "pass judgement" on the way that relationship appears to the outside world.

Men tend to be rewarded for personal accomplishment. Regardless of how you personally calculate success as a man, the common criteria would be a good physique, personal strength, financial success, ability to obtain a good-looking spouse, nice house, well-behaved children, etc. These are all personal accomplishments that are either achieved or not achieved through the man's personal behavior.

Women, on the other hand, tend to be evaluated based on the accomplishments of their family less than their own performance. Historically, that nice house, etc. would have been provided by the husband. If the husband is a jerk, people might look down on the wife. If a man cheats, many people see that as a failure on the wife's part. Badly behaved children tend to be perceived as a failure on the mother's part more than the father. Conversely, most women are proud if their husbands or children achieve success.

So, your relationship with your wife, right or wrong, occurs in a social context, even when you're by yourselves. Anything that you do, right or wrong, could have social ramifications for her. If you buy her a nice piece of jewelry, what's the first thing she's going to do? Show it off to her friends. If you're very attentive to her needs, she will relay that to her peer group. That's a notch in her belt. If you're not, that will get relayed eventually too; and it works against her social standing.

You might be thinking, "Why would she gossip about something that makes her look bad? And why would she gossip about something personal about our lives like whether I throw my socks on the floor!"

First, remember that "Romance = Attention." Sharing negative information about their relationship may get them much needed attention from their peers. Also, in a group of women who have similar complaints, this may create a bond between them that provides a form of satisfaction. If everyone in the group has similar complaints, there is no loss of social standing. There's no issue with that. In that situation the "worst" husband can actually be an asset, but we would not recommend your focusing on meeting this "need."

Second, female language is based on offering support. When a female shares information, there's an expectation that the other women in the group will offer similar information as a form of support. The part they have in common with men is that they probably go to their peers to blow off steam. If a woman needs to vent and says something like, "I'm so angry with my husband, he's such a slob!" Then her friends are socially obligated to offer feedback on their spouses as well. While that's the most important aspect of the conversation, the women who are also married to "slobs" don't get any brownie points for that. The woman who can say, "Well, I can't complain about my husband. He always puts his socks in the laundry" has the highest standing in the pack.

The best take-away from this concept is to try to keep in mind that everything you do for/to your wife can affect her social standing. From small acts of superior communication and teamwork to grand gestures, how you conduct yourself provides raw material for her movement up the social ladder. You can maximize this effect by making sure there is an overt social aspect when you make a grand gesture. Rather than meeting her at the door with flowers, send them to her work. Instead of choosing an isolated restaurant for a romantic meal, take her out when there's a good possibility a friend might be present. If she's on the phone with a friend, choose that time to let her know that you love and value her.

Coming out of this chapter, you need to keep in mind:

1. Women may not accurately express their feelings; little things may mean a lot.

2. There may be a hidden agenda in a marriage that if not addressed could turn into a time bomb.

3. Listen to all feedback, especially sarcasm, and make a habit of finding out how she really feels.

4. Women are social creatures who, right or wrong, will be judged based on your behavior.

Chapter Three

Can You Give Her What She Wants?
Every Time?

Can't Get Satisfaction

What is "satisfaction?" That is, how can we scientifically describe a state of being satisfied? We propose that satisfaction is based on how accurately a need is met. From that we extrapolate that satisfaction is then also dependent upon how accurately you can define that need based on the concept that it would be difficult to meet a need without having a good, specific idea of what that need entails.

Both men and women may have trouble articulating needs. Regardless of gender, it might be easy to express the fact that you're hungry. But will any food satisfy that hunger? Maybe. Or maybe if we were to offer you some brussels sprouts, you would quickly refine that need to something more specific like pizza or a hamburger.

If you don't understand your own need, how can you express it to someone else? If your wife doesn't understand her own needs, or isn't able to express them in suffient detail, how can you satisfy them and her?

It's Not Having What You Want, It's Wanting What You Have

There's no book in the world that can help you find out what a person really wants; he or she must learn to express their needs more succinctly. What you can do to help that process is to encourage your spouse to be more accurate about her needs by asking for more information. We will delve deeper into this in later chapters. For now, we encourage you to ask questions. When your spouse articulates a need, particularly one you are expected to satisfy, ask her to clarify. Her degree of satisfaction will be directly related to how well you understand what she wants. It logically follows that unless you ask for clarification, you're unlikely to be able to perform up to par.

If we're not interested in resolving inefficient conversation in this chapter, you might be confused about what we are interested in resolving. Put simply, the point of this chapter is to teach you how to manage expectations.

We find it unlikely that a woman would want to get rid of a relationship with which she's satisfied. Also, we believe when a couple is satisfied with a situation, both parties will have a better experience. To that end, it's not only important what you do in the context of that relationship but also to make sure that you manage expectations to ensure the perception of what you do is properly received.

Suppose we told you that a young man walking by an elderly woman pushed her off the curb. You're probably horrified, right? Doesn't sound like a nice young man. Most likely a young hoodlum assaulting an elderly lady. You have that perception because, in most cultures, the word "young" implies someone who is less than mature, possibly lacks respect for their elders, may have an over-inflated sense of ego. "Man" indicating "male" has, right or wrong, a connotation of someone who is more attentive to action than feelings.

Now suppose we tell you that right after this happened a kid on a skateboard whizzed through the space where the elderly woman had been standing. How do you feel about the scenario now? Just having that knowledge suddenly transforms an assault on the elderly by a delinquent into the actions of a hero.

This is what we mean when we're talking about managing expectations. It's not enough to do the right thing and to assume that the people evaluating that perception will correctly interpret it. Both before and after you act, you need to make sure the perception of what you do is going to be correct.

The writers of this book include a married couple. One Thanksgiving, the husband took all the guests into the living room to play video games thinking this would be best for his wife who was trying to cook dinner. She finished the dinner and served it. About a year later, during a major fight where many grievances were aired, she had essentially the following feedback:

"Last Thanksgiving, I called you a number of times to come into the kitchen and cook your recipe for your grandmother's stuffing. You just ignored me, and I had to do it myself when I was trying to cook other dishes. I was counting on you to do your part and you let me down."

His response was essentially this:

"I was entertaining the guests to keep them from disrupting you in the kitchen. I didn't hear you call me. When you called me for dinner, I was irritated that you had gone ahead and made my stuffing. It's a family recipe, I have a special way of making it, and I only get to have it on Thanksgiving. The fact that you made it deprived me of an experience I was really looking forward to having."

Both parties had a negative experience. What they discovered as the cause of this problem was the assumption that the husband had heard his wife calling him. In this case, the husband has ADHD which caused him to hyper-focus on the game. In that state, a bomb could have gone off in the kitchen and he might not have noticed. So, he worked during that argument to manage expectations in the future, telling his wife, "I have ADHD. I would never knowingly ignore you. In future, please just tap me on the shoulder or physically touch me to get my attention so that I can be responsive towards you."

Now this was a situation where there is a learning disability involved, but we think it's a great example. How your spouse perceives what you do can greatly influence her interpretation of any outcome. We think it's best not to wait until after something occurs but to be proactive in your approach.

Whether it's something small like whether you respond to verbal cues, or something big like what kind of a house you're going to buy, it's best to have a conversation about the outcome. If there is a limiting condition, like a learning disability, that is going to affect your performance, let your spouse know early. We think if you have a genuine limitation, most spouses will be very understanding of that. However, we urge you to make sure it's a valid limitation. For example, if you're going to be on a business trip to the middle of a desert for eighteen weeks before her birthday and you genuinely won't be able to buy her a present, we think she would understand. If you articulate the limitation in advance, her expectations will be appropriate to the situation and she's much more likely to be satisfied. Whether you grab something from the airport gift shop or put some sand in a bottle, she's much more likely to be satisfied with a small gift if her expectation was no gift.

While you shouldn't dictate to your spouse, the more information she has on what she can expect from you, the smoother things will go. If possible, negotiating an outcome beforehand is the ideal. If that's not possible, make sure you check back with her after something happens to make sure there's mutual agreement. You can have a "debrief" about almost any topic from whether dinner went well to whether she liked a gift. Invite her feedback on whatever just occurred. "Did you have a good dinner, honey?" Make sure you listen to what she says. If you don't understand, ask for clarification.

What you don't want to do is assume your spouse, out of love, will perceive your actions in the right manner. If she doesn't, this doesn't mean your spouse has negative emotions toward you or lacks positive emotions. Perception is always influenced by underlying assumptions which might not be obvious to you. For example, one of the authors worked in sales for a short time. At a morning sales meeting, a volunteer was taken out of the room. The rest of the associates were told the volunteer would come back in and act out sitting on a toilet. When the volunteer returned, he strutted to the front of the room, swung one leg over the "toilet" and with a swagger, assumed a confident seat on his throne then looked confused and hurt to see his colleagues laughing hysterically. The volunteer had been told to enter the room and act out sitting on a motorcycle! But the difference in underlying assumptions regarding his actions made a huge difference in how they were received by the group, which was the point the organizers were trying to make.

By making sure your spouse always has all the information that she needs to interpret your behavior, you can avoid any misunderstands. For example, maybe you will decide to purchase her a small teddy bear for Valentine's day. You might have several reasons that you think are obvious: you don't have a lot of money, the house doesn't have room for a bunch of stuffed animals, etc. After giving the gift, there's nothing wrong with articulating that information. "I hope you liked your bear. I thought about buying you something bigger, but I chose this one because ...."

If You Don't Give In, You Might Just Be Ok

In the previous chapter, we mentioned that if you have what she perceives to be a negative character trait, even if she considers it a "deal breaker," you don't necessarily have to change. We also said that if your wife nags you, you don't necessarily have to do what she wants, when she wants it. Both issues can be addressed if you properly manage expectations.

Some negative character traits may be a "deal breaker" in the sense that if you don't change, she's willing to end the relationship. If she articulates that, then you need to listen to her and take that seriously. If someone is willing to communicate an ultimatum, then it just makes sense to respect the magnitude of what they're expressing. If you end up in that situation, all you can do is get as much clarification as you can and then decide if you're willing to meet the terms of the ultimatum. Perhaps in getting clarification you can negotiate a compromise. However, make sure the compromise is acceptable to both parties. If you get your wife to agree to a "compromise" that doesn't fundamentally change anything that's important to her, you haven't solved the problem. You've only delayed the break-up. In that case, stop wasting both her time and yours. It's time to move on.

However, maybe you can get clarification and ultimately negotiate a compromise. For example, maybe the deal breaker is that you smoke. What about this is a deal breaker? Is it that you smoke in the house and you can limit yourself to smoking outside in future? Is the problem that you smell of cigarette smoke and you can change your personal hygiene to address the problem? Is smoking really such a deal breaker that if you don't stop then the relationship ends? If that's the case, how quickly do you have to stop? The more information you can get to refine your understanding of the problem, the more likely you will be able to address it with a satisfying resolution. A deal breaker doesn't necessarily mean that you must change. Maybe she doesn't like you smoking because it costs money, and you can adjust your budget to address that underlying concern. But even if you don't change, what you *must* do is address her concerns and arrive at a solution that is as acceptable to her as it is to you.

She's A Woman, Not A Horse

We also said that if your wife nags you, you don't necessarily need to do what she's asking you to do, when she's asking you to do it.

Nagging is fundamentally a mismatch of expectations versus behavior. Generally, if someone is nagging you about doing something (or not doing something) it means that a) they have an expectation that you can/will do (or not do) that thing and b) they expected that expectation to be realized already.

We don't believe that anyone "likes" to nag another person. It's just as much work and just as annoying for the person nagging as the person being nagged. This most likely represents a failure on one or both parties to properly articulate expectations. However, if your spouse is nagging you, the one thing you shouldn't do is ignore it. Since it's no fun for her either, this can represent a source of resentment that will build up over time and cannot have a good outcome.

First, you need to determine if assumption a) is correct: is this something that you can/will (not) do or should (not) do? We would tend to think that in a nagging situation, there most likely needs to be an adjustment on this end which is typically achieved by changing the dynamics of the situation. For example, if your wife is nagging you to fix something, do you have the time/expertise to do that? Can you hire someone to do it instead? If she's nagging you to not put your feet on the coffee table, maybe the coffee table needs to be moved out of range? If you're leaving dishes in the living room, maybe there needs to be a rule about not eating in the living room? Look for something that can solve the underlying situation by changing the system so her need to have something done and your need not to be the person meeting that need can intersect.

You may also have to address the second assumption as well. In general, not only does this mean your spouse already anticipated the expectation to be realized, but we also think it tends to indicate that they believe you have had enough opportunity to accomplish it. We don't believe, for example, that if it was the husband's "chore" to take out the garbage on Sunday and if he were away for two weeks, that the wife would nag him about having missed performing the chore on the weekend he was away. If that is what is happening, there is some other kind of problem. We'll address this when we get to the subject of communication later in the book.

But if in fact the issue is with the timing, then what you need to do is evaluate that timing. If it was realistic, your wife is justified in believing this is something you could have and should have already accomplished. In that case, get 'er done! Next time, do a better job of coming to a mutual agreement as to deadlines. If not, you need to make her aware of the limitations that have prevented you from accomplishing the task. You also should negotiate a reasonable schedule for completion. Then it's up to you to stick with that schedule. If she's nagging about getting out of debt or buying a new house, maybe you can't make that happen now. Can you set up a schedule for saving money? Can you agree on some parameters where she can see real progress on the goal?

Ultimately when it comes to nagging, you're going to have to work with her to establish reasonable expectations. If you do that and meet the resulting expectations, this problem will disappear over time. When you demonstrate a pattern of predictable and reliable behavior of setting expectations and then meeting them, there will be no reason for your wife to nag you.

The take-aways for this chapter are as follows:

1. The more clearly needs are articulated, the better chance those needs can be satisfied.

2. Manage expectations by being clear and concise in advance about what will happen.

3. Manage expectations by checking after the fact to evaluate the reaction and ensure that your spouse perceives things the same way you do.

4. Nagging almost always indicates a need to re-examine the issue from the perspective of seeking to change the parameters in some way.

5. Once you have negotiated reasonable expectations with your spouse, you need to meet them.

Chapter Four

Is It Only A Matter Of Trust?

Trust is probably one of the most important aspects in any relationship. Once trust is gone, it's hard to rebuild. The good news is that if trust has been damaged, you can start rebuilding it right away. If you've never had it, you can still start building it right away. You don't have to wait for opportunities to build trust. You can create them daily until your relationship is rock solid with a trust foundation.

First, let's look at what trust really is: trust is confidence that someone will act in a way that is in line with what they have said they will do and the values they have articulated. Whenever you do what you say you will do, trust is strengthened. Whenever you don't do what you say you will do, trust breaks down.

It might sound very basic but it's one of the most important aspects of a relationship. We all fundamentally want to feel secure. Feeling secure means that we trust our circumstances.

For many couples, conversations about trust revolve around cataclysmic issues. Certainly, if one partner cheats that is a huge breach of trust. When you get married, you promise to be faithful and forsake all others forever. You say that this other person is the only person for you for the rest of your life. If you then take another lover, that's a very clear example of your actions not being congruent with your words.

But trust can break down from small daily actions as well. If you say you will take out the garbage on Sunday and don't, that negatively affects trust. Saying you will be home at six and arriving at seven also works to erode trust. No one feels comfortable in a relationship where they're not sure what's going to happen, so take every opportunity to build up trust seriously.

Count On Me

The first way to build trust is to demonstrate that you're dependable. Being dependable isn't dramatically different than being trustworthy: you're dependable if you do what you say you're going to do.

We believe that most people are basically dependable, although some people aren't. If you're not a basically dependable person, that will be up to you to address. People who routinely do not do what they say they're going to do usually have deeper issues like substance abuse, major depression, etc. Most people show up for work when they're supposed to, keep doctors' appointments, pay their bills and so on. If you have a major issue with following through on what you say you're going to do, then you probably need a little more help than you can get from a book. We suggest you talk about this with your spouse and come up with a plan to get help.

For the rest of us, being dependable isn't such a big deal. However, men often feel that their failures "count" more than their successes. Sure, you're on time for work every day but promise to fix the sink once and forget and it's game over, right?

The issue of dependability is a logical extension of the previous chapter on managing expectations and is going to leverage some of the same concepts.

First, you should work to make sure your spouse is recognizing how dependable you really are by articulating what you are going to do before you do it. This both manages her expectations and simultaneous raises your behavior into the spotlight so it can serve as an example of your dependability. Almost anything can serve as proof that you're dependable. "Honey, I'm going to go outside and walk the dog for about ten minutes. Then I'll come inside and watch television with you." Once you do that, poof! That's a point in your favor. Be forewarned, if you don't do exactly that, it's a point against you. The key is to rig the point system in your favor by being clear and specific in your articulation of what you plan to do. The other key is to not "promise" anything that there is any possibility you may not be able to do.

Because we live in an imperfect world, if you say you're going to do something, and you're not able to do it, you should let your spouse know as soon as possible. The best situation is if you let her know before the deadline for the activity. If a neighbor ambushes you in the back yard, text your spouse and let her know the walk is going to be longer than ten minutes. If you can't let her know before the deadline, you *must* let her know as soon as possible but no later than the first opportunity you have. In this situation, always start with an apology, "I'm sorry it took more than ten minutes, honey, Jones talked my ear off in the yard."

Some men might feel uncomfortable apologizing in this situation. This stems from a misunderstanding over what an apology constitutes. If apologizing makes you feel uncomfortable, most likely you feel an apology is an admission of guilt for an action that is wrong. Why should you apologize in this situation? It's not your *fault* Jones talked your ear off. If your spouse really loves you, why should it matter if it took you longer than ten minutes to walk the dog?

First, the reality is that you don't know, and you can't know, how much your behavior means to your spouse. We feel confident in assuming that everyone has had a moment of disappointment in their lives, probably in childhood. Think of a situation where your parents disappointed you. Disappointment can be related to someone just being unable to meet an expectation. You wanted a bike, and they couldn't afford to buy you one. We think it's more commonly related to a mismatch in emphasis. You really wanted to go to the park, but your parents decided not to take you. Children tend to forgive when you can't meet their expectations. We tend to remember very vividly where we didn't get what we wanted based on a values mismatch. Sometimes things that seem insignificant to one person are extremely significant to another. Never assume you know how important a subject is to another person and you will never go wrong.

Second, apologizing to someone doesn't have to be an acknowledgement of fault or guilt. It's all right to apologize for something that isn't your fault or even if you've done nothing wrong. What you're apologizing for is the way the person is feeling in case they blame you for that feeling. Even if you did nothing wrong, if someone else is feeling bad, that's not a good outcome. There shouldn't be any hesitation on your part to apologize for (possibly) making someone feel bad. What an apology really does in that situation is acknowledge that person's feelings and let them know that you empathize with them. We feel that there is no reason you can't empathize with another person under any circumstances without compromising your integrity. Suppose your spouse begins yelling at you, "I'm so upset! You said you would be home at six. When you didn't get here, I was worried! How dare you!" There shouldn't be any problem with saying, "I'm sorry the fact I was late made you feel worried and upset." That doesn't mean you're agreeing with the fact that you did something wrong. You can easily continue with, "I wanted to be home at six but there was an accident and they closed down the road for forty-five minutes. There's nothing I could have done differently to have been here by six."

Apologizing also serves to defuse almost any situation. To have an argument, there need to be two people with two opposing viewpoints. If you apologize for whatever is upsetting your spouse, it immediately relieves the tension and defuses the potential for a fight. Again, it doesn't mean you're giving in on a difference of opinion. If it's an emotional discussion, focus on the emotions. "I'm sorry my *action* made you feel *emotion*."

The second thing an apology conveys is an unspoken promise not to repeat the behavior. This is another aspect that can make some people reluctant to apologize. It can also be a source of frustration for the recipient of the apology if the behavior is repeated after the apology.

You can't apologize for behavior and then keep repeating the behavior. That's the antithesis of dependability and trust. By apologizing, you are implying you won't repeat the behavior. When you do, it negates the apology and serves to degrade trust. That's why when you apologize you need be clear what you're apologizing *for*, making it clear what your spouse can expect in the future. If there's really nothing you could have done better or different, make that clear, "I'm sorry I made you feel upset by being late. Of course, if I tell you I will be home at a specific time, I will always try to meet that goal. However, I can't control traffic. If I'm late, please understand it's due to something out of my control." And if that is always the case, then she will trust you.

A better solution is if you can turn this situation into a trust building opportunity. "I'm sorry I made you feel upset by being late but, unfortunately, I can't control traffic. It never occurred to me that you would be worried. In the future, I'll call you if I'm running late."

What you don't want to do is avoid the fact that you have disappointed her expectations. Either she will keep her disappointment to herself and bring it up at another time, "You don't care how I feel. The other day I was waiting for you to come back from walking the dog and you took a half hour instead of ten minutes!" Or, if she decides to call you on the behavior, she will be resentful because she will interpret your failure to address the issue as either negligence or a lack of caring. "I thought you said you would be back in ten minutes?" "Oh well, yeah, Jones caught me in the yard." What she's thinking is, "So, Jones is more important than me?" Instead, if you immediately address the discrepancy between the expectation you set and the reality, it reassures your spouse by letting them know that you're aware that you did not behave as you said you would, that her reaction is important to you, and that you would not behave that way if you had any other choice.

This may all feel trivial to most men. We don't think it is. Trust is built up over time based on patterns of behavior. If you don't take every chance you can to show how dependable and trustworthy you are, your spouse won't think of you in that way. We think most women prefer to be in a relationship with men they consider dependable. This provides security and assures them that they are the person their husband cares about most.

She Can Tell What You're Going To Do Before You Do It

The second important aspect of trust is predictability. If dependability addresses the concept that someone does what they say they are going to do, predictability addresses the fact that what they do is in accordance with their articulated values.

Predictability addresses the situations where you haven't articulated what you're going to do in advance or when your spouse is not around. If they trust you, they can accurately predict what you're going to do, and they feel secure. If they can't accurately predict your behavior, they don't feel secure; they don't "trust" you.

Predictability, the way we're using the word, doesn't mean always performing repetitive actions. We're not talking about a situation where every time you park the car you pull up the parking brake. Rather, we're talking about a pattern of behavior that is used to predict future behavior in an unanticipated situation.

One of the first things you need to address to achieve predictability and trust is to make sure your spouse understands your value system properly.

For example, let's say you and your spouse both agree that you value cleanliness; you both value a tidy home. However, every night you eat dinner in front of the television. After you're through eating, you place your dishes on the coffee table. In the morning, before you go to work, you remove the dishes and put them in the dishwasher. What does your spouse think of that? Does she trust that you value cleanliness?

It depends on how she defines cleanliness. If her interpretation of cleanliness is that before any transition in state everything is in its place, then most likely she trusts you. When you go to bed, the house hasn't changed state. You're both home. If you clean up before you go to work, before the state of the house changes, then you're good to go. If her definition of cleanliness is that everything is in its proper place as soon as you're done with it, then your spouse may perceive you as being a slob. She doesn't trust that you're a clean person, and that may cause anxiety. Then, whatever you do, she will be watching to see if you clean up after yourself in what she considers a timely manner. Eventually, this will spill over into other facets of life.

This is similar with couples as it regards fidelity. Some people define fidelity as not showing any interest in any other person. Others are fine with any level of showing interest if there's no activity with another person. If that's misunderstood, one spouse may look at attractive people or even flirt, causing the other spouse untold anxiety. They don't trust their spouse because there is a mismatch in the value system. This is directly related to managing expectations: it should be very clear what your value system is so your spouse can always know what to expect from you.

Once you've articulated that value system, it's important that your behavior is consistent with it. If you say that you prioritize saving money, then your spouse can trust that when presented with any situation where you can choose between spending money on a luxury and saving money, you will choose to save the money. She can "trust" you as it concerns money. Then if you suddenly go out after work and buy a big screen television, that damages trust. She thought she could predict your behavior but in fact, she couldn't. Have you ever heard someone say, "I never thought that person would do that!" What they are articulating is a betrayal because they thought they could predict the person's behavior in certain circumstances. Finding out that they made the wrong prediction makes them question how well they know that person which leads to a degradation in trust. If this happens frequently enough, the relationship will inevitably break down.

If you decide to act against your articulated value system, you want that big screen television, you absolutely *must* discuss this with your spouse first. Here predictability differs from dependability. If you say you're going to do something and can't meet that obligation, then you can let her know as soon as possible. This is acceptable because it's a deviation from a specific promise for a specific behavior. However, when you share a value system with your spouse it's an implied promise against an infinite amount of future behavior. If you break that implied promise, that's the hardest kind of trust to rebuild and the type that typically destroys a relationship. At a basic level, what you're communicating is that you don't have consistent values that govern your behavior which means you are completely unpredictable. Very few people will be comfortable in a relationship with someone like that.

If you don't discuss the departure from the norm in advance, then the best you can do is to address it before she confronts you, starting with an apology. Again, the most important aspect of "trust" is that your spouse can see a direct relationship between what you say and what you do.

Let Me Guess

If you don't work to make that connection, if your spouse constantly observes you saying one thing and doing another, she may not leave you. Some people will observe another person's behavior and try to construct an imagined "value system" for that person based on observable behavior.

This isn't good for two reasons. One, it will result in your being held to a standard of which you have no knowledge. Two, it can result in a perceived value system that's incorrect and may hurt you later on.

For example, let's say you haven't articulated your value system as it relates to yard work. You never said whether you value a clean yard or not. Or, perhaps you said you don't care if the yard is tidy or not. However, every Saturday you mow the lawn like clockwork. If you haven't articulated your value system, it is still realistic for your spouse to conclude that you value a tidy lawn. If you've said you don't care, your spouse will most likely assume that is not correct. Your actions bely your words. What's going to happen if suddenly you get busy and don't bother to mow? Your spouse will most likely be nervous. You're not adhering to the value system she constructed for you based on your pattern of behavior. Even if you originally told her you don't care, there's been a major behavior change from her perspective. What's new? What's wrong? It's a lot of anxiety she doesn't need to have.

There are very few people who don't benefit from a consistent, structured, predictable environment. Even people who supposedly thrive on chaos often have parts of their life that they appreciate being structured. The weekend backpacker who may relish an unexpected rainstorm will probably feel out of sorts if their employer doesn't direct deposit their check on time. Having clear and open communication with your spouse about your value system, and then meticulously behaving according to that value system, makes you predictable which in turn will inspire your spouse to trust you.

That doesn't mean there isn't room for creativity or spontaneity; to inspire trust you don't have to be a robot. But fundamentally, most women want to feel secure in a relationship and they feel secure when they feel confident that they know how their husbands will react. If you have good communication, if you're an expert in managing expectations, your wife will trust you and your relationship will flourish.

Rebuilding Trust

If you have already violated your partner's trust (or if they have violated yours) then you can rebuild trust by focusing on either dependability or predictability and increasing the frequency of demonstration. In this case, it's critical that you leave no room for doubt. If you have had an experience with your partner that demonstrates that you are untrustworthy, that person is going to be extra sensitive to your behavior. In a sense, you've used up any "slack" to which you might have been entitled; a simple apology isn't going to cut it. The only thing you can do is begin to act in a trustworthy manner as quickly and consistently as possible. Eventually, this pattern of trustworthy behavior will overcome your transgression. Don't be impatient with your spouse. If you were the transgressor, she is entitled to choose when she is willing to trust you again. If she was the transgressor, you are entitled to make that choice. The only thing you must do if you decide to stay in the relationship is to give her an opportunity to prove her trustworthiness. If either party is not willing to let the other rebuild trust, it's unlikely the relationship will survive.

For example, suppose you cheat on your wife. That's a major transgression on the predictability side of trust. When she finds out, she's not going to trust that she can predict your behavior when you're around women and not with her because when you got married, you articulated a value of fidelity and you didn't behave in accordance with that value. The only thing you can do is leverage dependability to try to rebuild that trust. Increase your contact with her. When you leave for work, let her know when you plan to arrive there and then text her to confirm you behaved as planned. Let her know what time you're going to take lunch and then let her know you took it on time. As you put down a pattern of dependable behavior it will restore trust which will eventually translate into predictability, security, trust and happiness.

Once broken, trust can be rebuilt. On the other hand, if you continuously attack trust, it's unlikely the relationship will survive. Be dependable. Be predictable. It's your best bet for a long and happy marriage.

Remember:

1. Trust is a foundational building block for a good relationship.

2. Trust is a confidence your spouse has that you will act the way you say you will act and that your actions will match your articulated values.

3. Trust is made up of dependability and predictability.

4. Dependability means she can count on you to do what you say you will do.

5. Predictability means she can reasonably predict how you will act in a given situation when she's not around based on your articulated values.

6. If you must deviate from what you have articulated, let her know in advance or at the very earliest opportunity: never make her confront you on the deviation.

7. Take every opportunity to build trust by clear, concise communication and managing expectations.

Chapter Five

Are We Communicating Yet?

For communication to happen there are three components: talking, listening and filters. All three are equally important and only by being aware of all three can you establish good communication with your wife.

Communication is one of the most important aspects of a good relationship.

One of the writers took a marriage course as an undergraduate. The priest, who had been a marriage counselor for two decades, was fond of saying, "If there's something you think you can't tell your spouse; if I told her this, she would leave me. Then tell her quickly and stop wasting her time because it's going to come out at some point."

Tell Her About It

The first thing you must decide is *when* to communicate. We agree with that priest's advice: choosing not to communicate forever is a bad decision. Secrets never stay secrets. On the other hand, timing is not to be undervalued. So carefully choosing when to communicate is important. In general, communication done in anger is rarely productive. It's better to think before you talk. A good rule of thumb is never hesitate to say something good. Never hesitate to delay something bad.

Romance=Attention.

Whenever it occurs to you to give your spouse a compliment or let her know you appreciate her behavior, follow that instinct. Conversely, if you find fault with her, that will have to come out as well. In that case, the key is to make sure you communicate the information in a way that's helpful and not hurtful. One of the writers had a grandmother who liked to say, "Say what you mean, mean what you say, but don't say it mean." Words to love by.

If You Can't Go For That

With negative feedback, the key is that it should be constructive. In order to be constructive, most people need to choose their words carefully. This is usually not possible in a moment of anger. So, delay the conversation until you've had a chance to plan what you'll say. Choose a time when your spouse will not feel the information is being shared as revenge or punishment. It's also important to make sure you have a fair, productive solution to share. It's not critical, but we think it's always preferable not to raise a problem until you have a solution. Even if that solution doesn't end up being THE solution, at least you proposed one. No one likes to be saddled unexpectedly with a problem to which there is no solution.

For example, let's say your spouse has a favorite recipe for lasagna which you hate. It's a family recipe. She loves it. The family loves it. You're the only one who hates it. You can't make her stop loving it because cooking that dish brings her untold pleasure because it reminds her of happy times in her childhood. This might be a situation where, because there's no solution, you decide not to mention it. What you cannot do is hold back information and then reveal it in anger. Let's say that after five years of not letting her know, the two of you get into a fight about home-cooked dinners. You should not yell, "And I've never liked your grandmother's lasagna!"

However, perhaps you realize during the fight that you desperately want to stop keeping this secret. First you need a solution. Let's say, in this case, you realize you go out to dinner with friends once a month as a "guys night out." So maybe the solution is that she could make the lasagna on that night. Then, pick a time when everything is going well to raise the subject. Make sure she knows you're not rejecting her. "Honey, I love you. But I don't love lasagne. I know how much this means to you. I would never want you to give up cooking it. What if you made it on the nights I go out with the guys?"

Many people don't like this concept because they don't want to spoil a good time by raising an issue. This is the optimum time. She's in a good mood and more likely to listen.

Filters

Of the three parts to communication, the one you have no control over is filters.

This is a term we just made up so, to the best of our knowledge, no one else uses that term.

By filters we mean a sort of lens through which whatever is said or heard will be processed.

Like it or not, everyone filters what they hear based on their past. How you were raised, every experience you've ever had; these things create a filter through which everything you see, hear, and speak is processed. In the song Blinded by the Light, there's a line that's commonly misheard as, "Wrapped up like a douche, another rumor in the night." The song was written by Bruce Springsteen, but the most popular version was performed by Manfred Mann who slightly altered the lyric to, "Revved up like a deuce, another runner in the night."[2] Filters are probably why this song is so commonly misheard. "Deuce" is a term for a 1932 automobile. This song was released in 1976. At that time, it's unlikely most listeners would know what a "deuce" was and connect "revved" to a car. It's also not a word used very often except perhaps in relation to gambling. When song lyrics are misunderstood, the mind automatically searches for a rhyming word; not many words rhyme with "deuce." Since the mind is substituting "douche" for "deuce" the brain tells us that if you sang it fast and didn't articulate well, "wrapped" makes the most sense. It starts with an "r" sound and ends with "ed" just like "revved." Plus, even guys know that many feminine products are wrapped at some time. In Hotel California, the Eagles use the word "spirit." ("I called up the Captain, 'Please bring me my wine,' And he said, 'We haven't had that spirit here since 1969.'"[3]) Does that word mean "wine" or does it refer to the "energy" that the speaker is exhibiting when he makes the request? Realistically, it could refer to either. Your interpretation

---

2   https://en.wikipedia.org/wiki/Blinded_by_the_Light
3   https://en.wikipedia.org/wiki/Hotel_California

is going to depend on your filter. (The writers remain in disagreement over this lyric.)

Our filters are unique to us as individuals, but they affect everything you say or hear. For example, in the Midwest the most common word for a sweet, carbonated beverage is "pop" as in, "Do you want pop with your burger?" In the Northeast, "pop" refers to a quick, unexpected blow, as in, "I was angry, so I popped him one." You can probably see how this could cause problems. A Midwesterner could say, "I'm going to give you a pop" and someone from the Northeast could easily interpret that as a threat. Of course, if these were friends, it might be that the person from the Northeast will just be confused. But in a neutral situation, or especially if the conversation is hostile, then it's might be perceived as a threat rather than a peace offering.

Since filters are unique, all you can do is try to be aware of your own filters and, if possible, theirs. If in doubt, ask for clarification.

Of course, the effect of filters is rarely as transparent as our examples but let's try one more for clarity.

Let's say you decided to say to your wife, "I prefer steak over lasagna." Ostensibly, you're just staying a fact. However, if your wife has a history of being verbally abused, she may well interpret this as meaning, "I hate your lasagna." She might also hear, "I think you're a lousy cook" even if you thought what you were saying had nothing to do with her cooking skills or possible lack thereof.

Filters come from experience and can also be influenced by the context. For example, perhaps no one at an antique car show would miss the Springsteen lyric. That's why you want to avoid giving negative information during an argument and instead deliver it in a calm, happy moment. If the information is already negative, you need the circumstances to offset that filter as much as possible.

Word Choice

This also factors into how important word choice can be. We think how something is said is almost as important as what is said.

So, when you choose words to convey negative emotions, it might be best to start by planning what you want to say. If you feel up to it, maybe try rehearsing in your head in advance so you can anticipate and listen to how it sounds before you say it.

On emotional topics, avoid strong emotionally charged words like *love* and *hate*. Once you open the conversation, there will be plenty of emotion without your adding any. Problems get solved better when you can talk about them rationally. This is part of the reason for not negotiating in the heat of the moment. So not "I hate your lasagna" or "I've never loved your lasagna" but maybe "Lasagna isn't my favorite food."

It's important that whatever you're discussing, your wife not feel attacked. You can accomplish this by focusing on yourself rather than her and by making the conversation about her actions not her being. Structure your feedback as, "When you do *action*, I feel *emotion*." This way she knows you're rejecting her behavior not her being. If you truly are rejecting her personally, then it's time to end the relationship. But if that were the case, why did you buy this book? So not "You're such a nag" or "I can't stand your nagging" but "When you nag me about something, it makes me feel unhappy (unloved, guilty, worthless, etc.)."

If you can't anticipate how your wife's filters will influence her interpretation of what you're saying, you can start the conversation by testing it. "What would you think if I told you that lasagna isn't my favorite meal?" Or, you can check in with her at any point during the conversation to get feedback on how she's interpreting what you said.

The most important thing is that she knows that a) you love her, b) you care about her feelings and c) you're not attacking her personally. A good technique for diffusing negative interpretations is to present your feelings as a personal issue and ask her help to solve it. Generally, when you ask for someone's help it's understood that you respect that person. "Lasagna isn't my favorite food. I love to see you cook it because I know how much you enjoy that. But because it's not a food that I like, when you cook it for dinner, I feel bad because if I don't pretend to love it, I'm worried you might feel rejected. On the other hand, not telling you my feelings makes me feel like I'm lying to you. How do you think I should resolve this?"

If in doubt, phrase the issue as your problem not hers. "I'm struggling with understanding why you nag me. I know it must mean that you need me to change, but I don't seem to be able to understand the underlying problem. Can you help me?"

You never know, your wife might also have hidden issues with whatever you're discussing. "When you nag me about something, it makes me feel unhappy." What if she turns around and says, "When I nag you, it makes me feel unhappy too." Then you can easily say, "Then why do you nag me?" And expect to get a good answer.

Which brings us to the third component of communication which is....

You Must Listen As Well As You Hear

Maybe it should go without saying that you must listen to what your partner has to say but that's surprisingly a challenging task for most people.

Particularly during an emotional conversation or an argument, it's human nature to be eager to get your turn to talk. But the truth is, you can either talk or listen but not both. One of the writers is a teacher and was horrified to learn that students take in about 60% of what is presented in class, which, if you think about it, is just a little better than half. That's not a good number! This is probably why most self-help books have so much repetition. Readers don't take in 100% of the information so they provide multiple examples, making their point several times to ensure the communication between the writer and the reader happens effectively. (For the record, we hope you will reread.) Many people spend the time when their partner is talking anticipating their turn to talk, either giving their partner non-verbal messages of impatience or running through their reply in their head. That's not listening. When you're not talking, you should give your partner your full attention. If you have trouble listening to what your wife says, try asking her questions. Then you might be more able to focus on her reply. Otherwise, make sure you're listening to her. Be sure she knows you care about her feelings and ideas.

Romance=Attention.

Listening=Attention

Therefore, logically, Romance=Listening.

When you first met her, you probably listened attentively to everything she had to say. You needed that information to grow the relationship. That stage can never end. If it does, the relationship stops growing. Relationships are either growing or atrophying. They don't just stay the same any more than people just stay the same. All the information she communicates is important intel you can use to strengthen your marriage. Knowing her feelings, her needs, her desires, her goals, and her fantasies are the key to being able to manage her expectations and be the prince. Never let her feel as if you're not listening and taking what she says seriously. As we've said before, behavior is not idle. If she's taking the time to give you information, that information is important if not in the moment, then at a later time; listen when you have the opportunity.

After you and your spouse finish talking, take some time to internalize the information. Summarize for yourself what she said and make an effort to store that in your memory. If you don't have a good memory, make some notes. There may be a test later, and you want to pass.

The next few chapters will build on this one. If you haven't really taken in the content of this chapter, reread it.

The take-aways are:

1. Good communication is critical for a healthy relationship.

2. Communication has three components: filters, talking and listening.

3. Filters affect the interpretation of the communication.

4. Filters come from the past and the circumstances: they can't be changed but they must be acknowledged and taken into consideration.

5. When you say something is as important as how: don't hesitate to give compliments, never respond in the moment in anger but also don't try to keep secrets from your wife. Everything comes out eventually.

6. Choose your words carefully: avoid words that add emotion needlessly or make your partner feel attacked.

7. Limit criticism to your partner's behavior not their personality by focusing on how their actions make you feel.

8. Be sure to listen to what your wife has to say; everything she chooses to communicate is important intel that you need to (re)build a strong relationship.

Chapter Six

Honesty; The Best Policy?

The quality of the communication with your spouse is going to depend on how honest you can be with her. If you're anticipating that we're going to tell you to be as honest as you can be, that's correct. We won't waste your time belaboring an obvious fact. Instead, let's spend some time talking about lies.

First, let's be clear about what type of lies we're not interested in exploring. We define "lie" as the communication of something that is factually untrue. Therefore, although this could be debated, we include both the circumstances where the person lying knows that what they're saying is untrue and the situations where they don't know that what they're saying is untrue or communication that by virtue of omission would lead any reasonable person to an untrue conclusion.

Within this wide scope, we're not going to address lies where the liar knows they are lying and their motivation is greed, to hide criminal behavior, or to deliberately, emotionally or physically, harm their spouse. If you or your spouse are lying for these reasons either the relationship needs to end, or you need professional mental health care. No self-help guide can address problems of that magnitude.

Nor are we going to address secrets maintained out of fear of rejection. At this point, we expect that we have adequately established that if there is something you think you can't tell your spouse out of fear of rejection, you should tell her and stop wasting time for both parties. We also hope you have an understanding of how important trust is and that one of the two main pillars of trust is predictability, which is your spouse's expectation that she can depend on you to act in line with your articulated value system. When you get married, some of the

59

implied meanings inherent in marriage is that you love your spouse, you do not want to see them harmed in any way, and that financially you are a single unit. So those topics should adequately address the types of lies we won't be discussing.

Unfortunately, even removing those categories, it still leaves a whole lot of lies to tell.

It's Not A Lie, It's A Fib

We believe that most people know lying is wrong, and yet, we also believe most people lie every day. Some people qualify these lies by using alternate terms like "fib" or "white lie." The use of these terms just tells us that the person knows they have uttered an untruth but believes, because no harm will come to the person receiving the lie, that it shouldn't "count."

All lies count.

This isn't a religious book, so we're not going to lecture you on morality from a religious perspective. In civil society, ethics constitute a set of rules that allow people to know what they can expect from others in certain situations. Your spouse most likely expects you to be truthful with them. When you lie, it undermines trust. Without trust, the relationship will eventually end.

One reason why married partners might tell lies is because they fear reprisal. Suppose each Wednesday, you go out to the bar for a drink with a group of male friends. You tell your wife no women are allowed because these friends don't like your wife. Why have you "lied?" Because if your wife comes, your friends will be annoyed. One week, one of your friends brings his new girlfriend. This time you "lie" by not mentioning this to your wife because she would be hurt.

It's true these kinds of lies function as a kind WD40 of relationships for some men, allowing them to avoid friction they believe will damage the relationship or to avoid friction with friends and family as it relates to your spouse. We think they're an IOU on problems that, when they hit, will carry with them interest that will make the issues so much larger the risk to the relationship just isn't worth it.

If any outside parties don't like your spouse, they don't like you. It may sound harsh, but it's a fact. Why did you get married? At a basic level, marriage is a legal and public institution that requires society to view the married couple as a single unit. Spouses aren't required to testify against each other in criminal court. When you file taxes, you file jointly. The world is supposed to see you as one unit. Anyone who refuses to respect that doesn't respect you. This marriage may be the worst mistake of your life, but it's your mistake to make. Even if your marriage doesn't last, we encourage you to really examine any friends who refuse to respect you by respecting your spouse. They don't have to like her; but if they value you, they won't make it difficult for you to be their friend when your wife is around.

One way to solve this issue is by not falling into the trap of being a different person when your spouse is not around. Everyone needs to vent sometimes. Negative feelings build up like helium in a balloon. Either you stop adding to the balloon, or you let a little out from time to time. Do yourself a favor; if you're not ready to discuss the issue with your spouse, hire a therapist. They get paid to be neutral and not repeat what you say. It's rare to have friends who value both members of a couple equally. Your friends and family most likely value you more than your spouse. You may vent to them and resolve the issue, moving on. Not so your confidents. They can't get resolution with your spouse. They don't have all the good experiences that you have had and will have with your spouse. They will remember your complaints long after you forget them. When you married your spouse, you effectively asked the world to see you as a unified entity. Any negative about her is a negative against you. Keep that information in the relationship. Never say anything behind your wife's back you would not say in front of her. If you don't follow this guidance, it's inevitable that something you say or do that you're hiding from her will get back to her. At best it will hurt her feelings. At worst, it will also damage trust and destroy the marriage.

Another reason to lie might be to save your spouse's feelings, either solicited or unsolicited.

Unsolicited white lies may have a variety of motivations. We think it all comes down to a pure motive of wanting to make your spouse feel happy. You spouse is telling you about how horrible her day has been and accidentally burns dinner. As she sets the charred remains on your plate, you bravely take a big bite, feign enjoyment and say, "But dinner came out great, honey. Thank you so much." We're not buying it, and neither will she. If you love this woman, surely there are any number of things you can say that are both true and buck her up. How about, "You've had a hard day. Let me have dinner delivered." Unsolicited white lies are easy to discover and what they tell your spouse is that you're not honest with her all the time. The intelligent person will naturally wonder what else you lie about, and there goes trust and your marriage.

Solicited white lies are harder to deal with. Typically, the solicitation is asking for a personal comment on her. "Does this dress make me look fat?" Most men are probably thinking, "There's no right answer. If she has to ask, she thinks it's yes. If I'm honest, I'm in trouble. If I'm not, I can always play the 'love is blind' card and I'll be in less trouble."

Wrong.

Any time your spouse solicits your opinion, it's an expression of trust. She's asking you to be her teammate. The rest of the world judges her without her permission. She's giving you permission, so don't blow that. Be honest but not mean. "Of course, I think you look great. But that's not the most flattering dress you own." "It's a lovely dress but if you're asking me if that dress flatters your figure, I don't think it does you justice." There are hundreds of ways of saying "yes" if that's your honest opinion. If you say "no" then what happens if she wears it and someone else tells her the dress makes her look like a blimp? Either you're a horrible judge of her attractiveness, in which case she won't trust your opinion, or you're a liar with all the attending problems with that assessment.

One last thing to address is overt lies told by giving an impartial truth. Everyone knows that lying is wrong, but it often seems as if people pretend that they're lawyers in a courtroom. Your friend's girlfriend attends the guys only night out. Your wife asks you who went, and you say, "Well, I went out with the usual group." Technically, even if your marriage was a court you couldn't be accused of perjury. As far as we're concerned, this is a lie. If it gets back to your wife, do you think your argument that you didn't technically lie is going to be compelling? If you have done this or do it in the future, we recommend against trying to defend yourself. Whether you try, "It slipped my mind" or "I didn't technically lie" it's only going to make you look like a bigger liar. Simply take responsibility, "I'm sorry I didn't tell you. I didn't want you to feel bad that another woman got to go when you didn't. I'm going to address it with my friend. Either you can come, or he won't bring his girlfriend again."

Overt lies are generally to avoid negative consequences or to proactively bring happiness to your wife. While both of those motives might be good motives, hopefully you can see that lying isn't a good way to achieve this.

You Don't Know What You Don't Know

Lies where the liar doesn't know they're telling a lie are tougher. How can you avoid telling a lie if you don't know you're lying?

We're not talking about a situation where there's no possible way for you to know it's not factually true. For example, if you have a variable rate mortgage and your wife asks you what the rate is; you give her an answer without knowing the rate has changed. We don't consider that a lie per se. We're talking about lies where you don't know you're giving the wrong information but it's reasonable to assume that you should. The types of lies that fit into this category usually occur because you are failing to be honest with yourself.

It's hard to think up examples but we'll try to get as close as we can. Let's say your boss belittles you all day. When you get home, your wife asks you what's wrong and you say, "My boss was bugging me all day and annoyed me." This might be the truth but it's probably not. More likely you're upset about feeling trapped, not being respected, etc. The fact that it's your boss behaving this way probably means what you're feeling goes deeper than annoyance. If you don't express those feelings, you have effectively lied.

This is true of your spouse as well. You can help her by listening to what she says and looking for patterns. Ask questions designed to get at the underlying problem, "Is that really what you're upset about?" You might feel that calling this a "lie" goes too far, and we might be stretching, but whatever you want to call it, these issues must also be addressed. You might not always realize when this is the situation, but we think most people know when this is going on. If nothing else, watch out for situations where you or your spouse become extra sensitive to certain questions. If one of you is feeling easily irritated or irritated out of proportion to the issue you think you're talking about, it probably signifies that you're not being honest about your true feelings either to yourself, or to your wife.

The take-aways from this chapter are:

1. Honesty is the best policy. A lack of honesty erodes trust and destroys marriages.

2. Lies told to avoid reprisal or just make your spouse feel good are ineffective. When discovered the reprisal or her negative reaction will be worse.

3. Whether solicited or unsolicited, white lies are still lies and should be avoided.

4. Lies of omission are also lies.

Chapter Seven

Can You Hear Me Now?

There's never a bad time to tell your wife, "I love you." But work, kids, the demand of running a home - all these things can make it hard to remember to let her know. Not everyone is great with words. Some people feel that their spouse should understand every act they do is an act of love. If you go to work, come home, pay the bills - shouldn't those things inherently be understood as expressions of love?

They should, but generally they aren't. That's why it's so important to manage expectations. If one of the ways you show your wife that you love her is by going to work or paying the bills, you must let her know that.

One of the authors had an eight-grade science teacher who defined entropy as "the natural tendency of the universe to tend towards disorder." If your marriage isn't getting stronger, it's getting weaker. That's why it's so important that you make every effort to make sure your spouse knows how important she is in your life. Unfortunately, you could tell her that you love her one hundred and fifty times a day, but that doesn't guarantee your marriage will be strong. The frequency of your loving communication is important, but the content has a great effect as well.

"I love you" is just a phrase. President Richard Nixon said, "I am not a crook", but that didn't make it true. The reality is that actions are more important than words. No matter what you say, if what you do contradicts that, your spouse won't trust that you're telling the truth.

First, try communicating more than just "I love you." Remember when you first met your wife? Most likely you talked about a lot of things. You told her about your past, your present, your hopes and dreams. Just telling your spouse about your day is an act of love. Listening to her tell you about her day is romance. The more time you spend communicating with your wife, the more loved she will feel. The more attentive to her needs you are, the more emotionally secure she will feel.

We believe women want a man who makes her his top priority. The way she knows she's your top priority is by how much attention you give her. If you spend more time on hobbies and friends, then she's not going to feel loved.

Many men might be thinking, "I don't have a lot of time. I leave for work early and work hard all day. When I come home, I'm tired. Weekends go fast. Can't she just know I love her?"

Sorry, Charlie. It doesn't work like that. The good news is, once you get into the habit, it's easy to let your spouse know how much they mean to you. And it doesn't take all that much time either.

A good rule of thumb is whenever you have a short period of time, reach out to your wife. In this age, there are so many quick and easy ways to contact your wife it shouldn't be an issue. When you wake up in the morning, greet your wife and give her a kiss. When you get to work, before you sit down at your desk, before you lock your car, send her an emoji kiss. If you get up to get a coffee, after you fill your mug, shoot her a text. If you run into an article on the Internet that reminds you of her, text her the link.

Short but frequent contact with your wife can go a long way toward helping her to understand and appreciate how much you love her. Every time you send a text it shows not only that you're thinking of her, but that you took your time to let her know. It's not the content of the text; it's the mental attention that it takes to make that connection that counts.

If for some reason you can't do this, maybe you work in a secure area, let her know when you can and cannot be in contact with her. Then, at the first opportunity you get, reach out to her. If you're not used to being in such constant contact, attach it to another activity. Maybe every time you eat, you'll reach out to her. Maybe it's every time you move from one location to another. Whatever "rule" you make up for yourself, let her know so she can appreciate your efforts.

Most people have very busy lives. If that's your situation, the most valuable gift you can give your wife is your undivided attention. Almost anything you value about your life can become an opportunity to communicate your love. If your spouse cooks, take a moment before one of the meals to let her know how much you appreciate that, "I want to thank you for making this wonderful meal, and I want you to know how happy I am to share it with you." Even if all you do is watch television together, you can easily just take a moment before the show comes on, "Honey, I want you to know how thankful I am to be here watching television with you tonight."

The key to making this successful is to just stop everything for a moment while you let her know your feelings. A formal moment of appreciation is worth much more than dozens of offhand "I love you" statements.

Public displays of affection tend to be very valuable. That doesn't mean that you have to kiss your wife in public if that makes you or her uncomfortable. Rather, if you know your wife is with colleagues or friends, make an extra effort to text her then. Or, when she's putting the kids to bed, you can let her know what a good job she's doing, "I'm so impressed with the way you make an effort to tuck the kids in every night. I want you to know how thankful I feel when I see how well you take care of our family." Not only will she know how much you appreciate her, your kids will know it too. In one comment, you are being both a good husband and a good father, and setting an example of both for your children.

When you get into the habit of communicating your feelings, this will come more naturally. The key is to let your wife know you love her and *why*. Everyone wants to feel noticed and appreciated. Love doesn't require grand gestures like flowers and diamonds. Simple moments of affection can be just as powerful.

If you're not good with words, is there something you can do or make to express your love? Jim Croce was a singer/songwriter; he expressed his love in a song. What's your talent? Even if you think you have none, pretty much everyone can write on a sticky pad. Leave her a note somewhere unexpected where she will find it; inside the refrigerator, the dishwasher, on her coffee mug, in her wallet, where she keeps her makeup, in a shoe. Is she active on social media? Post a message to her. Is she stuck at a desk all day? Send her an email. On her birthday, make a homemade birthday card and ask someone at her work to tape it to her monitor. The key to discovering opportunities to express your love is to understand that everything you or she does on any given day is an opportunity.

There is no specific rule for the frequency or content of how you should communicate your love to your spouse. But it is not possible to over-do it. Whenever you acknowledge that love to yourself, pass that information on to her. At a minimum this should be a daily event, but multiple times per day will be appreciated.

The take-aways from this chapter are:

1. Just saying "I love you" isn't sufficient to build a strong relationship.

2. Almost any communication can work to strengthen your marriage: share your feelings and make time to listen to hers.

3. Anything that happens during the day can be an opportunity for communicating love even if it's through a text, emoji or even a sticky note.

4. If you have trouble remembering to reach out, tie that instinct to a frequent occurrence such as every time you change location, take a coffee break or enjoy a meal.

5. If you are frequently unavailable, let her know when you expect to be available and communicate with her immediately after any period of unavailability.

6. Look at the lyrics of Billy Joel's song *Tell Her About It*. It's a great summary.

Chapter Eight

What Are You Really Saying?

"Fine! Go out with your friends!"

No discussion of communication would be complete without examining those times when communication is not to be taken at face value. While we could have chosen to address this in the chapter on honesty, we think this is characteristic of a different type of communication commonly called *metamessages*.

Metamessages are underlying messages communicated through other mechanisms besides the overt meaning of the words being used. This includes, but is not limited to, the sub-text of words, tone of voice, and body language.

Most men know that when a woman says, "Fine. Do *something*." What that really means is, "Everything is not fine. If you love me, you will do anything but *something*."

Unfortunately, not all metamessages are as easy to decode. Equally as unfortunate is the fact that most people do communicate in this way. Depending on where you or your spouse are from may also affect how much you use metamessages.

Metamessages go hand in hand with filters. For example, most of the authors are from New England. In this region of the country, being forward or aggressive in communication is considered rude. One of the authors lived in the Midwest for a while and was taken aback at the forwardness of communication. Any examples we can give might be an over-simplification so it's possible readers from either region might disagree, but it's for the sake of example only. Let's suppose someone from the Midwest might say, "You look terrible, are you sick?" A New England equivalent might be, "Are you feeling all right?

Maybe you're coming down with something?" Taking regional differences into account, they both said the same thing. We have friends from the South that tell us that the phrase "Bless their heart" can be used as an insult which wouldn't necessarily be obvious to someone from the Northeast as in, "Bless his heart, he really believes the moon is made of green cheese."

If you and your spouse come from different parts of the country, you're probably already aware of regional differences in metamessages.

However, there are major differences between the genders in terms of metamessages. While this is not necessarily true of all men and women, it is our job to generalize. And, in general, women make much more extensive use of metamessages than men do. This is not to say that men don't use metamessages. They certainly do. If a man is asked to do a chore and he responds, "Well, the game is coming on in five minutes" everyone tends to know that this means "I don't want to do that chore right now." But we feel that women make much more extensive use of metamessages and that these metamessages can be more difficult to decode.

If you've been implementing some of the advice in the previous chapters, this should help. Paying attention to your wife, encouraging honesty, and building trust, might make her less inclined to use metamessages. Metamessages may be used in situations where the person feels uncomfortable simply stating how they feel. However, they are also used for several other reasons. Many men feel women just want them to read their minds, and we don't disagree that, at times, this might be the most accurate interpretation. But whether fair or not, we'll try to give you the best information we can about how to decode metamessages as we think this is an important skill to develop.

If You Could Read My Mind, That Would Be Ideal

We think metamessages always indicate a lack of depth in the relationship and can be corrected by strengthening trust, honesty and communication. But being able to decode them successfully will help in all those areas. Metamessages break down into two types: ninja and tests.

The vast majority of metamessages are ninja metamessages. These tend to be used in situations where the woman either does not want to have a confrontation or negotiation, or they no longer want to have a confrontation or negotiation. The latter tend to be easier to decode, the most famous being "Fine. Whatever." Or, "You're going to do what you want to do anyway." Both are intended to indicate, "The conversation on this subject is over, and I expect you to agree that I have won." If you choose to disregard her perspective after she delivers one of these lines, woe unto you.

But many ninja messages are much more subtle. For example, your wife comes into the living room and says, "I don't know how you can stand to watch television in a room this cluttered." Most men will take this simply as a bizarre comment. Many may feel inclined to reply, probably with something along the lines of, "It doesn't bother me" or even worse, "Why? I can still see the screen." Unfortunately, they've missed the point. What this comment really meant was, "I believe the living room is a mess. You are responsible for the mess. You should clean it up. And you should clean it up *now*." If you don't, there's a very good possibility that, at some later date, there will be an argument where she says, "And I told you to clean up the living room, and you ignored me!" This will, of course, completely mystify you.

In this example, the message is delivered in this way because the wife doesn't want to have a discussion, most likely because she either doesn't think she will "win" the argument or because she doesn't want the confrontation. Either way, it's made to avoid an argument, discussion or negotiation. When this kind of message is delivered, the person delivering the message generally assumes (incorrectly) that the message has been received and an implicit agreement has been reached. If this is not true, the bitterness that builds up will accrue as if it was. If you fail to decode the metamessage, you most likely will be punished then or later, and like the law, ignorance will not be an adequate defense.

A "test" message is a little different. These tend to be more subtle. The sad thing about a "test" message is that it is almost always directed at the person most likely to fail the test. These messages tend to be little "traps" laid to confirm a negative opinion on a facet of a man's character that upsets the woman. They urge the man to be more extreme or overt in the behavior. The woman's purpose is to give the man the chance to deny or repudiate the behavior or trait. However, because of the subtlety, it's almost guaranteed to provoke the behavior instead. Again, the failure on the man's part will almost always be punished then or at a later point.

For example, a wife that has frequently exhibited insecurity over her husband's fidelity is sitting in a bar with her husband. She's insecure because when attractive women are around, he tends to look at them. She's mentioned this before. An attractive woman enters the bar and the wife says, "She's good looking. I bet you would have a good time if you slept with her." What she "wants" her husband to say is, "Oh no, honey, the only person I ever want to sleep with is you." However, because of the wording of her comment, the husband feels comfortable saying, "Yes, it would probably be fun to sleep with her." In his mind, this is simply a "what if" and the best way to respect his wife is to be honest. All he means is "Yes, I like sleeping with attractive women." What she hears is, "Yes, I'm interested in other women."

We want to be clear that we don't support either of these types of metamessages. But while many men might be thinking, "Why can't they just address things directly," we think accepting this form of communication as valid is a form of setting a good example. If you want her to accept you as you are, and she uses metamessages, start by accepting her as she is and then work to change it.

Spotting a metamessage is the main challenge. Women tend to notice them easily because they're taught to encode and decode them from a young age. Men are not trained for this. But the good news is that there are rules you can learn. You'll probably never be as fluent as your wife, but as you become more proficient, you'll find it gets easier.

There are three clues you should be on the lookout for. In all three circumstances you'll recognize it by the fact that it doesn't fit the topic or situation.

The first is body language. If your wife's body language is contrary to the topic or the situation, there's a good chance she's giving you metamessages. For example, if in the middle of a long argument she suddenly smiles and begins acting very sweet, that's a sign of trouble. Conversely, if in the middle of a social situation where everyone is having a good time your wife suddenly becomes upset, be on the lookout for a metamessage.

The second clue is tone of voice. For the word "fine" you must visualize it in a sentence. If it would be followed by a period, it's a metamessage. If it would be followed by a comma, it's not. For example, "Fine. *Message...*" is always a metamessage. "Fine, *message...*" is usually not. A longer than natural pause after the word also helps identify that everything is far from "fine."

Tone of voice is always important. Pay more attention to negative tones indicating frustration, irritation, depression, and particularly sarcasm. Many people love sarcasm and dry humor. Even if that's your favorite method of communication, we recommend trying to cut it from your toolbox in the context of a relationship. Sarcasm is always a sign of a metamessage. Anger or sadness of tone is almost always an indicator as well. For example, if your wife says, "I guess you probably want to go out with the guys on Wednesday like you usually do" and her tone is sad, that's a metamessage. Any tone that's at odds with the conversation or situation most likely has hidden meaning.

The third is word choice. That's the best description we can give you. If the overt meaning of what she says is out of line with the flow of conversation or with her general character (beliefs) suspect a metamessage.

For example, the wife in the bar clearly values fidelity and has made enough comments in the past that the husband knows she disapproves of him looking at attractive women. A wife who regularly talks about who is attractive or not and jokes about extramarital sex is probably not communicating more than the overt meaning of the comment. If you're having a discussion with your wife on clutter and she makes a comment about the living room, it's probably just an observation. If she walks into the living room and makes the comment either when no conversation exists or as an abrupt change of subject, that's a metamessage. To go back to the regional examples, if you made the comment, "I have a terrible headache" and the New Englander says, "Are you feeling all right? Maybe you're coming down with something?" Then it's probably an honest comment. If it's right after greeting you or represents an abrupt shift in the conversation, it's a metamessage.

I Love The Way You Lie

After spotting a metamessage, decoding them is easy. The "real" message is either the exact opposite of what is being said or is an extremely shallow version of a deep message. "Probably," "guess," "most likely," and other verbal clues of insecurity tend to signal a test; they're a solicitation for you to contradict whatever is being said. "I guess you probably want to go out with the guys on Wednesday like you usually do" is code for at least, "I would prefer you don't go out with the guys this Wednesday." It may also signify, "I would prefer you don't go out with the guys on any Wednesday." In either case, what she wants is to hear you say is you won't go. "Fine, do what you want" is code for "don't do *whatever we were talking about that you want to do.*"

Messages that represent a shallow version of a deeper issue are harder to decode but not impossible. "You used to send me flowers, but now you don't" is unlikely to be about flowers. Flowers, in American culture, represent caring and romance. What this really means is, "I don't feel loved, and I would like you to be more demonstrative.

No, I Won't Discuss It

Metamessages are intended to be the final word in a conversation. Whether overt or subtle, they're intended to end a subject even if that subject hasn't even been openly raised in conversation.

This doesn't mean you have to agree or obey. If you don't agree or want to obey, you must recognize the underlying message and get her to enter into the confrontation/negotiation/discussion. "I don't know how you can stand to watch television in a room this cluttered." The best reply is, "It doesn't bother me. Does it bother you? Would you like me to (help) clean it?" "She's good looking. I bet you would have a good time if you slept with her." "Yes, she is good looking and I'm sure I would have a great time with her if I wasn't married. Are you worried about my looking at other women? I can assure you I only 'have eyes' for you."

The uber metamessage behind all metamessages is that your spouse doesn't feel that you're paying her enough attention. She doesn't trust you enough to feel safe discussing the topic overtly because she doesn't trust your reaction. She believes she has a superior reason why she should "win" that argument which justifies this approach. The only way you can truly end this method of (unhealthy) communication is by rendering it obsolete. Pay more attention to her needs and have better communication to reduce the topics she feels must be addressed. Build trust so that it's more likely she will have a genuine conversation with you when she has needs that are not being met. Some couples may feel this method of communication via metamessages is more "natural" and comfortable for them. In our experience, it's much more satisfying to have a relationship based on open and honest, not to mention overt, communication. Once you get used to just one level of meaning, rather than having to "decode" messages, we think you will both come to prefer it.

Fight To The Death: Not

One reason your wife might not feel safe discussing a subject or doesn't trust what your reaction might be is if when you argue, your reactions are extreme. Men are expected to offer solutions and to defend those solutions rigorously. Women don't work like that and offering a solution may even irritate them. Also, in an argument, men tend to fight harder in the short term. Men don't usually have as much tolerance as it relates to emotion. Emotionally, men tend to be "sprinters". There's a lot of emotion for a short period of time and then they seek relief from the stimulation. Women are more like "long distance runners". They can withstand a lot of emotion for longer periods of time and may even crave that. If you feel like your wife wears you down in conversations where the two of you disagree, then you may tend to come out strong to avoid a long conversation.

But while women often have the stamina to stay in an emotional conversation much longer, they also typically do not purposely seek confrontation. If every time there's a discussion, you react strongly then that feels more like conflict than friendly debate. If your wife feels like whenever she offers constructive criticism, you offer conflict, then she won't feel comfortable having that discussion. That doesn't mean she'll stop having those feelings. It just makes it more likely she will use metamessages for the subjects that she doesn't consider open to debate.

If you tend to react emotionally to feedback, try to get control of your feelings. People who "win" arguments by using superior strength or emotion can usually be described as "bully," not "loving husband." Rather than trying to resolve the issue quickly by expressing a lot of emotion, control the length of the conversation by communicating efficiently in a way that makes her feel comfortable. Then, you can have a resolution that pleases you both without making either feel that the conversation was the equivalent of verbal dentistry.

Now You Tell Me

One final word on sarcasm and dry humor. Plenty of people like exchanging barbs with their significant others. For women, perhaps even negative attention is better than nothing. For men, the challenge of creating witty zingers may satisfy their need for a puzzle or a challenge. Or maybe for both of you, it's just habit. But this type of verbal sparring is like children playing rough in a school yard. It's inevitable someone will go too far, and someone else will get hurt. If you're "joking" like this with your wife, only two people can possibly get hurt. We presume both of them are important to you. Don't do something that can't turn out well. If your wife enjoys this kind of humor, how do you really feel about it? She may be reluctant at first to break out of the habit. We're sure you'll be in for some snarky comments on your new leaf. Just let her know clearly and kindly that you love her so much that you've decided that you don't want to say anything negative about her, even as a joke. We feel sure that when she gets over the shock of the change, you will both be rewarded.

The take-aways from this chapter are:

1. Metamessages are messages communicated by tone, body language or word choice that contradict the overt meaning of what's being expressed.

2. They are used to avoid confrontation or negotiation and achieve a "win" in conversation.

3. They can be deadly to a relationship because they're symptoms of a deeper problem.

4. The key to recognizing metamessages is by observing something out of line with the topic or situation.

5. Failing to recognize them will always be punished.

6. The short term "fix" is to bring the topic up into overt conversation. The long-term "fix" is to work on the deeper problem.

Chapter Nine

Me Or All The Guys You've Loved Before?

Now that we've talked about filters and metamessages, we can talk about the role that experience plays in a relationship.

No disrespect meant to people who suffer from real PTSD: we all have a mild form of it coming out of any relationship. For that matter, our childhood experiences also play into how we behave as adults. Understanding how your wife's childhood and previous relationships affect your marriage can help you understand and manage challenges that arise from these sources.

It's going to be impossible to address the effects of what has come before you if you don't know what those experiences meant to your wife. Start by making sure you have the information you need. How did your wife view her parents' relationship?

At the risk of being too trite, many people either recreate their parents' relationship or actively try to create a relationship that "corrects" whatever they felt the issues were. So, you need to know what she liked and didn't like about her family growing up.

So too every relationship before this one has a role to play. You must understand what attracted her to the guys before you. What does she come back to again and again about those relationships? Why did they end?

It's not enough to just listen to what she says about these subjects. What's more important is what she says about how those events made her feel. When someone either wants to recreate an environment or avoid recreating that environment, what they really want is to either replicate or avoid is the feelings they associate with those times. Often people don't relate the feelings but rather the facts. You can determine the feelings either by asking or by extrapolating, or a combination of both.

Naturally, we can't replicate psychoanalysis in this book. There's a reason why people pay thousands of dollars over the course of many years for this service. But you can try to apply the principles within the context of your relationship so you have greater understanding of what your wife really wants or needs.

For example, suppose a wife says this, "My parents had a good relationship. What I really liked about my home growing up was that my parents didn't argue. If there was a fight, it ended quickly. When I met my first boyfriend, I was really attracted to him because he was strong and confident. But after a while, he became bossy and controlling; and I had to break up with him."

There's a wealth of information in that little paragraph. First, the fact that her parents didn't argue doesn't mean they had a great relationship. That's a child's interpretation of their relationship. If there were any fights, they ended quickly. That also doesn't mean that there was resolution but rather that the kids were not aware of any further conflict. So, as confirmed by her statements about her first relationship, she's attracted to people she considers strong. Most likely what she's really attracted to is feeling secure. That sense of security is fostered by people who come off as strong and confident. It's threatened by any sense of conflict because that wasn't allowed when she was growing up. This is probably a woman who makes extensive use of metamessages. But she ended her previous relationship because she doesn't like feeling controlled.

This would be a tough relationship to maintain. This woman would want her husband to help her to feel secure by being a "take-charge" person who isn't controlling. That's a tough line to walk. If her husband is struggling with the relationship, we would advise him to always avoid arguments. The key to forging a strong relationship would be to carefully raise subjects in a calm, rational manner. When discussing emotional issues, maintain a calm tone. Be firm yet loving in standing up for yourself but very respectful of her wants and needs. We never recommend raising your voice, but we understand that everyone has emotions. With this woman, it would be important to avoid expressing them in an overly-passionate manner. She probably doesn't like negotiation. Simple disagreements, even about small things like where to go for dinner, could be perceived as conflict. She may be reluctant to express her real needs so her husband would have to work to figure out what she wants.

Let's try one more just to get a good sense of what we mean. Suppose what she said was this, "What I liked best about my first husband was that he was very romantic. The reason we broke up was that he spent too much time at the bowling alley. I'm pretty sure he was cheating on me. My second husband was just a horrible person. Whenever he got drunk, he would assault me. Finally, I had to get a restraining order. His only redeeming quality was that he never forgot my birthday. I always got a nice gift, a beautiful card, and breakfast in bed. My father was nothing like either of them. He wasn't abusive or romantic. He was a classic blue-collar worker who got up early every morning and went to work. At night, when he came home, his dinner was on the table exactly at 5:30 pm. Then he went into the living room to watch television. I don't know what my mother got out of the relationship, but she stuck by him."

At first glance, it looks like none of these relationships have anything in common. That's not true. First, we can tell that this woman absolutely believes that Romance=Attention. Because she didn't feel her father gave her mother enough attention, abandonment is a hot button. We can't tell if her first husband really cheated on her. What it does tells us is that when the attention faded, she moved on. To stay in a relationship with her, she needs to feel secure. It would be important to connect with her frequently. She married her second husband, despite his being abusive, most likely because negative attention was better than no attention. The effort he expended on her birthday was enough to give her hope that with enough love she could transform him into a prince. There's even a little bit of nostalgia in her tone, more regret than we can hear in what she says about her first marriage. This is a woman who doesn't want to recreate her parents' relationship and she won't stand being set aside for any reason. Her husband will need to make sure she always feels loved and wanted, avoiding giving the impression of taking anything she does for granted.

It's not our expectation that everyone can address all the issues and baggage their spouse brings into a relationship. But sometimes just knowing how to avoid pushing their buttons is valuable. If you listen to your spouse's stories and think about the underlying themes, you'll never know when that information might come in handy. If nothing else, she will appreciate the attention you pay to her.

The great themes of life are not so many and varied. We all want to feel secure, loved, the object of attention and affection. We all want to avoid negative emotions like abandonment and abuse. Always strive to be the prince! If you fall a little short, most often she will forgive you if you genuinely did your best. If you sit back on your laurels and revel in your frog status, you are missing a much deeper intimacy that could be yours and hers.

It's not easy to recognize when something from your spouse's past is affecting the present. This is one of the few topics where we're struggling to give a "rule" that men can follow. In this case, we think anything approximating a "rule" would be similar to the same rules for metamessages. If your spouse's reaction is incongruent with the situation, then you should consider the fact that the emotion might be coming from her connecting the current situation to something in her past. In this sense, the comparison to PTSD is the most useful. Why do people who went through wars seek to avoid fireworks? Because the sound of gunpowder exploding connects them back to the emotions they felt at an earlier time when they heard that sound. So too, if something going on in your relationship causes your spouse to connect back to an earlier (unpleasant) situation on an emotional level, she may react to those (past) circumstances instead of genuinely engaging with the current situation.

For example, taking the second "wife" we described above, let's say her husband is working on a project around the home. He accidentally hits his thumb with a hammer. Jumping up, he begins swearing and eventually throws the hammer down on the ground. Because his demeanor is similar to the wife's abusive second husband, the wife may have a panic attack or some other extreme reaction even though her current husband is not drunk, is not angry with her, and is not threatening her in any way. If his behavior is similar enough to the abusive ex-husband, she may react as if she's being threatened which would be emotionally painful for both parties.

If this happens, the only action you can take is to emotionally diffuse the situation. Acknowledge her feelings and provide comfort; give her a hug, a kiss, hold her – whatever is natural for

82

your relationship. Then, when the moment is over and she feels secure, encourage her to talk about what happened. See if you can mutually arrive at a point where she no longer connects you with the behavior that triggers her negative response. While this may not be possible, what you're trying to avoid is her emotionally attaching you to that earlier (unpleasant) experience. Unless you can get her to separate you from the past, you will carry the burden for the men who have come before you. Unless you truly are exactly like them, this is not your burden to carry. We feel confident that if you help your wife explore what's happening in a safe and respectful manner, she will agree.

The take-aways from this chapter are:

1. We all carry the baggage of our past. Listen to your wife for clues to her deepest heart's desires and the "buttons" you should never push.

2. In addition to what she says, look for patterns that might reveal underlying emotions.

3. If her reaction is out of proportion to the current situation, it may be that she's reacting to something in the past.

4. If in fact a reaction is to something that happened in the past and not the present, comfort your wife and encourage her to explore her emotions so she doesn't create a permanent connection between you and the past.

Chapter Ten

Did I Really Just Say That?

In his song, "The Stranger," Billy Joel talks about everyone having a sort of "stranger" lurking inside them that they don't share with their spouse but who can appear at any time. While we love the song, we don't necessarily agree. The stranger in the song is not buried far below the surface. In real life, we think "the stranger" is a facet of the personality that's always present. If that part of your personality or your spouse's personality comes as a surprise in the moments when it becomes predominant, we feel this is due to a failure to achieve true intimacy which ultimately can be traced to a failure to communicate.

Only now that we've been through filters, metamessages and how the past affects the present, can we talk about how to deal effectively with these challenges to good communication. If you have excellent communication with your spouse, you will have a very deep level of intimacy which dramatically reduces the chance there will even be a stranger inside of them. No matter how good the marriage, we remain separate individuals. No one can share everything they think and feel. But when a couple truly shares what is inside their hearts and minds with each other, then there shouldn't be many surprises. And certainly if one spouse trusts the other to listen to what they're saying, if they feel that they can predict how that spouse will react to whatever the revelation, then they will gradually reveal those things that, in less-honest relationships, become "secrets" the revelation of which sometimes derails or destroys the marriage.

At this point it should be obvious why miscommunication, which is really one of the major causes of the breakdown of relationships, can happen so easily. After the initial period of intense attention to each other fades, couples fall into a pattern that assumes the bulk of communication has occurred. You've shared your life stories and your feelings, culminating in that moment when you exchanged vows before family and friends, becoming one in the eyes of the world. True communication, with the attendant attention it requires, moves into a maintenance phase which, for many couples, is probably quite boring. Most people (thankfully) don't have jobs that are filled with drama and exciting developments that threaten their lifestyle. The couple's (shared) social circle of friends and family, including children, probably don't provide much fodder requiring extensive communication. It's interesting to note that in pre-married life, drama that requires sharing information is the foundation for romance and intimacy. After marriage (or cohabitation, if that precedes marriage) these topics would more properly be called stressors that threaten the union. As an aside, we think that is the basis of situation comedies like Three's Company, Cheers, Friends and The Big Bang Theory. They allow viewers to vicariously participate in drama without stress, because the drama has no ability to threaten the family. If your life is like a sit-com, you are probably neither amused nor entertained; and talking about it most likely doesn't count as intimacy or romance. This does make sense though. Talking about stressors involves giving the attention of both parties to the stressor and not to each other, which is the antithesis of romance if Romance=Attention.

We don't think it's a coincidence at all that the stage at which communication moves into maintenance is the same stage at which people usually complain that romance faded.

Further, filters - the lens through which communication is interpreted, combined with metamessages which rely on context to reverse the overt meaning of the words, play into the traps laid for us by our pasts. When communication moves into the maintenance phase, it's no longer happening with the attention to detail lavished during the pre-marital phase. For better or for worse, many people in the world are raised to believe marriage is the big finale — the gold medal, the grand relationship prize. Prior to marriage, many people are on their best behavior because their lover is not "tied" to the relationship. That subliminal goal of marriage that lurks inside the psyche inspires many people to work through issues that threaten the relationship. Despite the high rate of divorce in the modern era, after marriage there often comes a kind of dependency or assumption that the marriage will continue regardless of the effort (not) expended.

What Have I Done?

As the need to share information fades into the familiar routine of life, we think both partners need to be willing to keep communication fresh and interesting. But this book is aimed at husbands, not wives, so we'll try to keep our discussion specific.

First, spend some time thinking about the content of your communication. What do you talk about? Is it work, kids, and money, not necessarily in that order? What can you talk about that will be fresh and new?

This doesn't mean you should manufacture some drama in any area of your life. We think there's nothing wrong with having a "boring" life. We hope all of our readers have stable lives where all of their goals are met on a timely basis. Rather, what we mean is how can you find novel topics of communication in routine activities?

The stereotypical "date" is dinner and a movie. We think there's a reason for this. A shared dinner provides so much pre-movie content for discussion; how did your food taste? Was it good or bad? Is it your favorite or not? How was the restaurant/wait person/fellow diners? This carries through to the excitement of buying snacks until the movie which then provides the post-movie discussion palate. (Or not; one of the authors took a date to see Schindler's List. The relationship ended when she leaned over to ask, "Did this really happened?")

We believe almost anything in your current life can provide this type of entertainment. If your spouse cooks, where did she get her recipe? Was there any issue in the preparation from buying groceries to getting the food on the table? (For the record, while we have referenced women preparing food a number of times, the authors include multiple men who cook and who are excited to share their methods with the women they love.) Even traffic can be a source of engaging conversation whether you're relating getting stuck in traffic or bemoaning being cut off.

The key is to take the events of everyday (boring) life that you do not share with your spouse, and (presumably) they do not share with you and share them. While your wife is sharing the minutia of her day, be sure you listen attentively and interact with her. If you do, that's the kind of attention that will equal romance. Your attention will eventually inspire your wife to feel excited to relate these incidents to you. And even if right now you are shaking your head thinking, "That sounds boring" you may find that when you see your wife excited and animated about interacting with you, your opinion changes.

If you really have nothing to talk about, have a "date" in front of the television. Every night. Spend your evenings with the "tube" if that's what you like. But after you decide you're finished for the evening, leave time to talk about what you saw. Do you agree with a character/situation? What have you "learned" (if anything) or is that a certain amount of time in your life you can never recover? Sometimes the worst shows and movies make for the best bonding.

What Are You Talking About?

One of the primary ways to avoid miscommunication is through active listening. Active listening encompasses a whole set of behaviors, many of which we've already discussed, listening attentively, giving the person your undivided attention, avoiding anticipating the conclusion thus arriving at an erroneous conclusion. The aspect we're interested in here is the art of the paraphrase.

Whether your wife is communicating overtly or through metamessages, a paraphrase always works. It's the best tool you can have in your communication "toolbox." We will warn you that some women may be initially annoyed when you start trying to cultivate this habit or may be suspicious that there are ulterior motives. She may see this as a verbal "trap" being laid for her.

She's right.

But you're not wrong for using it. Over time, it can become as natural as breathing to you, and it can (no joke) save your marriage.

If your wife is initially resistant to a paraphrase, you might want to discuss it with her first. We suggest something along these lines, "Honey, it seems to me that sometimes we miscommunicate. Either I don't do exactly what you want, or I miss some things that you may think are obvious." Notice you're putting the burden on yourself. This new technique is not arising out of a "problem" with her but a failure on your part which is preventing you from being the best husband you can be. The beauty of this is that you're being one thousand percent honest. Although this may be resulting from the way she communicates (and the goal is not to assign blame; it could be her or it could be you. As the authors of a book, we don't know.) regardless of the cause, it is resulting in your failure to meet her needs, and you are proactively putting her on notice that you intend to be the best husband you can be. "So, in order to ensure that I know what you want from me, I'm going to ask you to confirm my understanding. That way not only will I be more likely to satisfy your needs, but over time I may be able to refine my ability to understand and then I won't need this technique as much." Again, all completely true.

Now, how does this work? Basically, whenever she asks you to do something, makes a comment, tells a story - in short, whenever she communicates ANYTHING you are going to paraphrase what she said and ask her to confirm it. We suggest that if you're having a lot of trouble in your marriage, use this for everything. Then, as you begin to get a feel for where you communicate well, you can back off on that subject and reserve it for the areas where you (plural) need work as a couple.

We would even suggest you might want to use the same phrase every time. If she gets annoyed, just tell her that's your "checking" phrase. When you use it, it's because you're trying to improve as a husband, and you hope she will indulge you.

For example, suppose your wife uses a lot of metamessages. We'll take the example of the wife who comes into the living room out of the blue and says, "I don't know how you can watch tv with all this clutter." Even if you sincerely think she's just making a comment, you can check it. "Let me make sure I understand you; I hear you saying you can't understand how I can watch the television with the room being cluttered? Because my immediate reaction is that there's an unobstructed view from the couch." If it's really just a comment, she'll laugh. If not, she will be forced to articulate the metamessage; "No, I'm saying this room is a pig sty, and I don't understand how you can sit there and not want to clean it up!"

Don't be afraid to go for round two! "Ok. Let me make sure I understand you. You think I should want to clean it up?" "Yes!" "Does that mean you want me to clean it up?" If she says, "Yes." Bingo! Now the topic is open to negotiation. If not, still bingo!

She can't come back later and accuse you of not cleaning the room because you have a verbal commitment to the fact that she does not expect you to clean it.

Suppose she's telling you a story about her past. "My parents had a great marriage, they never argued." Perfect. "Hang on a minute, honey. Let me make sure I understand. Are you saying that you feel a great marriage is one where people never argue?" Don't lose the opportunity to get her to explain herself more fully. Is it just a symptom of a great relationship or is it a critical ingredient to having a great relationship? What does she mean by "argue?" Does that mean "never disagree" or "never disagree in public" or "never disagree over trivial matters?" Find out what her filters and needs really are. As an added bonus, this is all attention which means it's all romance.

How about, "So, you'll be home by six?" Jump in, "Yes. But let me make sure I understand you; you expect me home by six? What if I'm delayed?" (Managing expectations.) "Someone said my boss was looking for me (I heard traffic is backed up, I'm tired and I expect to drive slow, etc) do you want me to text you? Or should I just come home as quickly as possible? Do you have anything planned that a delay would disrupt?"

"So, I guess you're going to go out with the guys again on Wednesday." "You sound a little sad. Let me make sure I understand you. Are you disappointed I will be going out with the guys this Wednesday, or does it bother you I have a 'guys night out?'"

The possibilities are endless. The great thing about this technique is that it allows you to get the issues out into the conversation. It also allows you to make a verbal "contract" with your wife regarding expectations. If there's an issue, you can always come back later and use this as your defense. "When I asked you to clarify, I was being sincere. I truly thought *something*. There's no way I could have understood you meant/wanted/expected *something else*." Once you institute this as a communication method that becomes familiar, there's no reason for her to resent this. Yes, you are asking her to commit to what she's communicating in a way you haven't in the past. But your motives are pure. You do want to be the best husband you can be. Both of you may become more sensitive to the sources of discontent in your marriage. This will enable you to work on them.

Context Is Everything

As you work on communication, the one thing you must be aware of is context. Even if you're not the master of metamessages, she probably is – be on the lookout for situations where she's receiving metamessages you didn't intend to send. For example, suppose you say, "I can't find anything to wear." If you're standing beside a full hamper of dirty clothes, she may hear, "I want you to do the laundry." Her response, "You need to do your own darn laundry" isn't out of line. But if that's not what you intended to communicate then you'll probably be flabbergasted. When there's a reaction that's out of line with the situation, it could be metamessages you're sending, or it could be past experiences. Either way, check in. "Let me make sure I understand. You're upset I don't do my own laundry? I'm not sure where that's coming from. Can you explain why you're making this comment right now?"

Even if the comment is not a complete surprise, there's never a bad time to paraphrase. At 4:45 pm you're sitting on the couch and make the comment, "It's almost time for dinner." She says, "Fine. I'll make dinner." Check in. "Let me make sure I understand. It seems as if you think I was asking you to make dinner? I just meant to make a comment on the time, but I can tell by your reply that you think I was saying something more."

Let us say this again! You can't overuse this technique! We can't imagine any harm can come from wanting to make sure that you understand what just happened in a conversation. If your wife is resistant to this technique, try to explain your goals to her and get her buy-in. We think it will be worth it in the end.

The take-aways from this chapter are:

1. Communication is critical in a relationship. Always find fresh opportunities to connect in everyday activities.

2. Use the paraphrase technique to improve understanding and establish a verbal contract to avoid later frustration.

3. You can't over-use the paraphrase technique. If your wife is resistant, explain the motive and use consistent verbal clues to help her help you use paraphrasing to ensure you meet her needs.

Chapter Eleven

Baby Can I Drive Your Car?

While some people lend more weight to words than action, we don't agree. We think the best indication of how someone is feeling or what they intend can be determined by looking at their actions. We all have friends we could go without talking to for a long period. What makes them treasured is the knowledge that, if we needed them, they would be there. Not that they *say* they would support you, but that they would *do* whatever was necessary to help you.

If you've come this far, you should have a good idea of how to communicate effectively. We know from our discussion of trust that empty apologies can keep a marriage going for only so long. In a way, they're worse than not apologizing at all. They're like giving a hockey player a shot of adrenaline to keep him on the ice after a fracture. The long-term consequences will be much worse than the original injury.

What brought you into this marriage was the concept that married life would meet you and your partner's needs better than being single. What will keep it going strong is if that math continues to work out in favor of the relationship. When what's better for an individual is to be out of the relationship, it will soon die. You cannot indefinitely postpone the end of something that is hurting one of the participants. But if you have mastered the topics we've discussed up until this point, we think you've done everything you can do to stack the odds in your favor.

We questioned whether to simply end after the last chapter. But there are some points to clarify after all just to give you every edge you can get.

Our topic here is action. In that context, let's discuss needs fulfillment and the social order.

At the beginning of the book, we asked you to accept that action is never without purpose. Even actions that seem to be random make sense to the doer. We know that, particularly for women, communication occurs in a very definite context which itself lends additional meaning. The same is true of actions. What you do or don't do adds to the filter used to interpret both what you do and say, so it pays to be as aware of your actions as your words.

This was never intended to be a how-to book on romance. Our thesis is that

Romance=Attention.

For that reason, small conversations and minor actions add up to something that is much greater than the sum of the parts. We believe your wife is more likely to divorce you over leaving your socks on the floor every day (if that bugs her) than for one massive mistake.

Not all women work like this, just like not all men lack skills or understanding in the areas we've highlighted. It's the nature of the business that we deal in stereotypes.

Because of this, we would be disingenuous if we started to list everything the authors (both male and female) feel are actions that your wife will find attractive or redeeming. Not every woman wants to have the door held for her or be treated to a free meal. The men in our group range from classic gentlemen to free-spirited thinkers, the women the same. So, what concrete rules can we take-away from a chapter about actions?

Plenty.

It's The Little Things

Paraphrasing works so well because not only does it avoid misunderstandings by creating an unambiguous verbal contract, it shows someone in the moment that you're listening to them and taking in what they're saying. That demonstrates in a very real way that you are paying attention to them.

But what if what they're talking about isn't something you can or should act on in the moment? The only way you can prove that you valued and retained what they said is to act on it when the time is right.

At the start, if this isn't something you do already, begin with obvious action items. Suppose your wife shares the following information with you, "I appreciate the fact that you take out the garbage every Monday morning, but it makes me nervous. What if they come early one week? I wish you would put it out Sunday night like everyone else does." Your instinct may be to resist this. You have your reasons. If everyone else jumps off a bridge, should you do that too?

When your wife has an issue with you or vice versa, we recommend that before you decide on a course of action, think about what this means to you. Every time you fail to meet a need that your spouse articulates, it's a black mark against the relationship. No specific black mark kills the marriage, but a critical mass of them can. Is this something you want to go to bat for? Is it really such a big deal to put the garbage out at night instead of in the morning? Compare the negatives from your perspective to the positives of knowing you have pleased your spouse.

Let's assume this is no big deal. Now you *must* live up to this. Even if you didn't acknowledge what she said or verbally agree to comply, now that she's voiced her feelings, every week you will either demonstrate your love or demonstrate your lack of caring. So, you need to put a reminder in your phone or whatever it takes. On Sunday night, get that garbage out to the curb. You might be shocked at the amount of pleasure and gratitude it inspires. Please understand your wife's gratitude isn't for the act of putting out the garbage. It's because you heard her concerns, internalized them, and changed your behavior to accommodate her. Nothing says, "I love you" as effectively as that sequence of events.

Once you become used to reacting to the important things your wife articulates, you can move on to more subtle things. For example, suppose you're watching television with your wife one night and a commercial comes on for a restaurant. As you watch mouth-watering visions of food flow across the screen, your wife says, "Oh that looks so good!"

You have a few choices at this point. You can check in, "Let me make sure I understand. Are you saying you'd like to go to that restaurant (have that dish for dinner)?" If you feel secure in knowing that either of those would be true, then you could skip the check in. Make a note of the restaurant and then make reservations or pick up some take-out one night to surprise her. You could take her out to eat anywhere and that's nice, but when she realizes how well you were paying attention to her off-hand comment and how you acted on it, she should be very pleased. Suppose you can't afford that specific restaurant? Find the closest thing you can afford and then make the connection verbally. "I hope you like it here, honey. I wanted to take you to that fancy restaurant we saw on TV, but it's just not in the budget. This place looked like the closest thing I could find. Are you happy or would you like me to keep looking?" Of course, she's happy. She has the most important thing of all; you. Plus, you now have plenty of fresh topics for communicating your feelings with each other.

Some men might be thinking, "It sounds like you expect me to hang on her every word and cater to her every whim."

Not at all.

If whatever the issue is turns out to be worth disappointing her over, that's fine. Just make sure you discuss that. Suppose you decide not to put the trash out at night. That very next Sunday night, let her know why. "Honey, I know it's Sunday night, and I know if I put the trash out right now it would make you happy." You can discuss a subject in the moment, but in this case, waiting until Sunday night to explain your decision makes it clear that you listened to her and understood her. Your decision not to take out the trash is just that, a decision. It's not laziness or because you forgot. So, having that conversation at the time you would be acting proves that this is deliberate. "However, I've decided I'm going to put the trash out tomorrow. As much as I love to see you happy and to avoid making you nervous, my reason is...." If you are making a conscious decision to do something your wife has gone through the effort of articulating that she prefers you not to do (or vice versa), at the very least you should give her a reason why you're making that decision. If you don't then the "reason" is because you don't love her. And no, that you loved her enough to marry her is not a one-time endless proof. The vows you took were words uttered at a big party held in your honor. If your actions contradict those words often enough, she won't trust you. It's all downhill from there. Maybe your reason is, "...because I've noticed on multiple occasions that wild animals get into the trash on the street and make a big mess. By putting the trash out tomorrow morning, I can be sure that it will go from the shed to the curb to the truck without causing any issues." If the situation permits, if you must disappoint your wife, try offering a compromise or a "consolation prize." So perhaps, in this situation, you tell her you're going to get up extra early on Monday to make sure it doesn't miss the pickup. Or, maybe you're able to pull up the town's website and you can prove to her that it won't be picked up before a certain time. Anything you can do to address her concerns will go a long way.

We think that most spouses of either sex can stand a little disappointment from time to time. They also love you. What's most important is your spouse does not feel you are ignoring her in any way. That's why, especially if you're going to choose to not accommodate her wishes, you should make sure she knows that you have understood her, you would accommodate her if you could, and let her know why you're choosing not to do so. If your wife tries to renegotiate, be open to that. Remember, a "win" for you that doesn't truly address her feelings is really a loss. Also, be careful in this situation to make sure she really doesn't have lasting discontent over the issue. Even if there are no specific signs of metamessages, we recommend you check in at the end of the discussion. "Are you really all right with my putting the trash out Monday morning, or are you just giving in to make me happy? I would much rather know your real feelings than end the discussion."

If it's really an issue for her, sometimes it's better to be wrong and let her come to that conclusion. "Because I'm fine with getting up right now and putting the trash out. However, you get home before sunset and I get home after, so if animals throw trash around the street, are you ok with cleaning it up?"

If she says she really cares about this and she wants that trash out Sunday night, what's the worst that can happen? There are only two possible outcomes: nothing ever happens, and she was right. She's ecstatic you listened to her, you acted on her wishes, and that she was right. Or, the trash gets dumped onto the street. (DO NOT SAY, "I told you so.") She's ecstatic that you listened to her, you acted on her wishes and she's mortified she was wrong. She's much less likely to fight you on any issue you stick to your guns on in the future and she may even try to make it up to you. (If you say, "I told you so," you just lost all that good will. No one likes a sore winner.) Either way, you win and the only risk you take is having to pick up some litter in the worst-case scenario.

There may be situations where the risk is much higher. We're not saying that if your wife wants to withdraw your entire retirement savings to buy scratch lottery cards that you should give in to please her if you don't agree with spending the money that way. What we're saying is that we believe the majority of situations where there's a conflict probably aren't life or death (or retirement) issues, and you should make sure your actions are always reflecting the love you feel for her.

This is why small problems snowball and are (sometimes) more dangerous than big ones. Suppose that one time you do something that really upsets and disappoints her. It's a "big" issue, but you apologize and truly never do it again. Every day that goes by that you never do it again, you're building up love by proving you respect her, and she can trust you. Compare that to the situation where your wife makes a small request of you to change the way you do a daily task. Well, if she thinks you ignored her, every single day your behavior is upsetting her. That means every day that new irritation is being added to all the days before. How long before that buildup becomes toxic? That's why it's so important, if you can't accommodate her, that you get to the point where you both agree that the outcome is respectful and loving to both parties.

The Post-Action Game Show

About actions, we want to take this time to reiterate a point made several chapters back. Women are, for the most part, more affected by their peer group than men. This is because women tend to get "ranked" socially based as much or more on the actions of their family than on their own actions.

This is not to imply that your wife is just waiting for privacy so she can regale her friends with your shortcomings. However, when she does get together with her friends, if she doesn't have anything good to relate, that's a major problem. Even if she stays silent while her friends brag (or complain) about the behavior of their spouses, in that situation, her having to be silent speaks volumes.

Suppose your wife has two good friends named A and B. They get together. A says, "My husband is driving me crazy. He doesn't listen to a word I say. If I ask him to do something, it never gets done. I asked him to make sure our son finished his homework and the next day I got an email from the teacher saying it never got done." B says, "Not my husband. If I even hint, I need something done, it's done practically before I finish talking. I asked him to walk the dog and I was carrying on talking to him and turned around and found the house empty. He and the dog were long gone." (Note: this behavior on Mr. B's part may be used as a negative example in a different conversation; he should have let Mrs. B know he was leaving.)

Now it's your wife's turn. Do you want her to be silent? That implies your behavior is so shameful it can't even be related. Should she just make a declaration that you're wonderful and she loves you? Without "proof" the assumption will be that you are horrible, but your wife is just too loyal to you to tell her friends the truth. They will give her major props; you just created your two worst enemies. The problem is the metamessage. Not offering an example is out of line in this conversation. Your wife's contribution, according to the societal expectations in this situation, should match what the other women are sharing in content and structure. Failing to meet them verbally with an equivalent is suspect. No one is going to assume your wife is holding her tongue because you're just too wonderful to talk about. Sticking with the trash example, your wife can come out on top either way. "My husband absolutely listens to me. I told him it upsets me that he waits until Monday morning to take out the trash and every Sunday since, it's out at the curb before nightfall." "My husband absolutely listens to me. I wanted him to take the trash out Sunday evenings instead of Monday mornings. He took a few days to think about it, then he explained to me that he had heard and understood what I wanted. He doesn't take the trash out Sunday night. We talked and he has a great reason for waiting, but it was so wonderful how concerned he was that I knew that he had listened to me and valued me. I know if there wasn't a good reason to put it out Monday morning, that trash would have been out Sunday night. And I'm so proud about how smart he is: it never occurred to me that putting the trash out early wasn't a good thing."

Now they probably want to hear all about your trash analysis so they can go home and test their husbands to see if Mr. A and Mr. B are as smart as you are.

If you find this extreme or think we're being snarky, we're not. We challenge you to ask your wife about this. There may be women whose peer groups don't work like this, but if there are, they're few and far between.

What About Me?

We did want to take a short moment here to talk about your needs. Everything we're saying about how you should treat her is also true of how she should treat you. If your wife doesn't treat you with the same care and consideration we're advising you to give her, it doesn't necessarily mean she doesn't love you. There may be reasons behind her behavior.

But you have every right, and in fact, a responsibility, to ask her to treat you as nicely as you treat her.

Some women may never have been in relationships where there is good communication. They may be used to the verbal abuse of a toxic relationship. Or, she may verbally be very loving, but her behavior belies her words.

You can and should ask your wife to have good communication with you and to treat you in a kind and loving manner. We do intend to publish a companion book for women, but much of what's in this book is just as applicable to women as to men. If your wife mistreats you, that's a cause for concern. While you work to change the relationship, protect yourself physically, financially, and emotionally.

Unfortunately, some men are just as invested in The Frog Prince as many women. They believe if she treats him like a frog, all he needs to do is keep acting like a prince and one day he'll get the magic kiss that will make it all perfect. It's one thing if your wife privately thinks you're acting like a frog and is plotting to make you her prince. It's something completely different if she treats you like a frog and seems to believe you could never be a prince. If this is the case, choose very specific behaviors and talk with her about them over time. It's usually impractical to have one big blowout. And generic feedback hurts more than it helps. Don't lose your cool and yell, "You don't respect me!" Find a neutral time to bring up specific issues, "It hurts my feelings when we're in public and you say, 'He's not the sharpest tool in the shed.'"

If your wife refuses to listen to your concerns, act on them, or provide satisfactory reasons as to why she won't change her behavior, we suggest you seek help either from a female relative or a mental health professional. We specifically mention a female relative because we're catering for the fact that no matter how wonderful a book we've written, maybe there's something going on with your wife that you just don't understand. Women do tend to share information with each other. Maybe that person can provide insight into the issue. If not, then maybe you need couples counseling. Everyone has a right to be respected and treated well in their marriage. The authors include members of both sexes who have tried to "fix" toxic relationships by being the best that they can be. The underlying pattern is that if your spouse is absolutely determined not to meet you halfway, that's an alarming signal and you probably need help to resolve it. At the very least, you need to protect yourself. If everything works out in the end, you have made yourself a stronger part of the whole. If it doesn't, then you can recover better. For either spouse, it is never unloving or disrespectful to the other to take care of yourself. If your spouse has an issue with that, there's something major going on that requires immediate professional help.

The take-aways from this chapter are:

1. Actions speak louder than words.

2. Often little things are disproportionately important in word and deed. Be sure your actions reinforce your active listening skills.

3. Think carefully before denying a "request" from your wife. If you must say no, make sure she understands why and agrees the resolution reflects mutual respect and will result in mutual content.

4. Avoid any action that makes your wife feel you are ignoring her. This is anti-romance and bad for the marriage.

5. Right or wrong, women are social creatures. They may be ranked on your performance in the marriage. Regardless of whether you can accommodate her wishes, be sure your actions give her bragging rights.

6. You have every right to expect as much kindness, effort, and love from your wife as you're willing to give.

7. If your wife won't meet you halfway, seek help to address any issues and protect yourself while you do so.

Chapter Twelve

Is That Really A Problem?

We could probably write a whole book on problem-solving. Maybe one day we will, but we felt the optimal amount for this book was one solid chapter. Not only do we need to talk about the differences between the genders, but we also want to mention some of the different approaches to problem solving. How you solve problems within the scope of your marriage will also depend on your values and how you work as a team.

Men tend to be problem-solvers. One of the authors recently called his father with a request for advice. The father listened patiently and gave advice. At one point in the conversation it would have been clear that the son could use some financial help, which the father offered. We think this is a great example of how men in general work. At no point did the son ask for financial help. However, in articulating a problem that could be resolved that way, the father naturally made that offer.

While the writer was happy about this (the metamessage was "I love you, son, and I'm willing to help") unfortunately, this same male instinct often irritates women.

Among men, articulating a problem is an invitation to the other person to help solve it. Very quickly, a "group think" evolves that might include debate as to which resolution is more effective. During this debate, there are (usually) never hard feelings over a difference of opinion. The "rule" is whoever can best defend his perspective is the one who possesses the best solution. Why would you offer your friend a solution you yourself are not willing to defend? On the other hand, if you do offer your friend a solution and they reject it, there may be no debate. That too is acceptable. However, the most important point is that it's never inappropriate to offer a solution.

This most likely comes from a historic, or possibly even pre-historic, society. In a hunter-gatherer society, men, as the hunters, need to exchange solutions for solving the very specific problem of bagging game. Leisure time, such as a lunch break on the hunt, would be spent exchanging information about the best solutions for hunting. In this situation, it's important that the best solution "win." Men would be expected to provide proof and argue for their solution because people's lives depend on the group achieving the "best" (objectively) solution. There can't be hard feelings because there can't be any impediment to the sharing and choice of the best answer. So, in a strictly male environment, not only is there no problem with offering a solution, it's expected.

Women, as we mentioned, have a completely different communication system. When a woman shares a problem, her primary goal is (usually) to solicit support. (Support is not synonymous with a solution.) Just as the degree of solution offered by male friends may differ depending on the degree of friendship, the type of support offered may also differ among women friends. Women may offer each other suggestions, but they rarely offer solutions. This is actually a huge difference. Typically, unless the friend verbally invites an offer of a solution, or the women are very close to each other, they don't suggest solutions.

In a historical context, this makes sense. With matters like hunting, there are a relatively limited amount of decisions. Are we hunting an animal that is typically a predator or prey? Is it a solitary animal or is it usually in a herd or pack? Is it bigger than us or smaller?

By contrast, gatherers have a lot more permutations to track. Just the category of berries will probably have more combinations than game. Comparatively speaking, it's much more likely to run into something unusual as a gatherer than as a hunter. We believe this might be why women tend to listen to all the information being shared, whereas men tend to interrupt conversations more than women. It's important that every gatherer be prepared to make his or her own decision because there are far too many situations for which an existing solution just won't fit. Not to mention that hunters probably don't have a lot of time each day to socialize, Gatherers would have more opportunity. Therefore, the ability to manage complex social interactions, caring for the feelings of the other people in the group, and making sure there isn't contention, would be much more important for gatherers than for hunters. While offering advice and support is important, it would also be important to help other gatherers develop their decision-making skills while offering information in the form of advice that the recipient could choose to take or leave.

Let's look at how this might play out. Consider the following example. A male is having difficulty at work. His boss gives him a poor review which results in a less than stellar raise.

Now that man is among male friends and relates the scenario. One would expect the guys to offer feedback like this:

Friend A: "That sucks. You should just go right into his office and tell him where he can shove his crappy raise."

Friend B: "No, don't do that. They'll fire you. Just dust off your resume and start sending it out."

Friend A: "No, you need to have a talk with this guy and let him know if this continues, you're out of there."

Principle: "I don't think either of those are good ideas. Maybe I deserved the crummy review. I'm thinking the best way to play it is to keep my head down and try harder this year."

The conversation can continue all night like this with each participant defending his proposed solution.

Now let's look at the exact same situation but with all women.

Friend A: "That sucks. That must have made you feel so bad. Have you considered talking with the boss to see if there's anything you can do?"

Friend B: "It sounds like they don't appreciate you anymore, and after all your hard work. Can you survive on that raise? Would you be better off looking for another job?"

Friend A: "Is that too drastic? Shouldn't she start with talking to the boss? If that doesn't work, she can always re-evaluate the system then."

Principle: "You guys are the best. No, I already know what I'm going to do. My boss made some valid points. The evaluation wasn't horribly unfair. I'm going to try to stay off the radar and by next year, it should be fine."

At this point there may be another couple of rounds of sympathy, but that's it. The women friends are not going to debate it. The metamessage from their friend is that she has a solution and the topic is closed. They primarily offered advice and that advice was shot down. So that part is over.

Now, we know people of both sexes who could easily say either of the parts. But in general, we feel that men are raised to offer "solutions" and women to offer support and "advice."

So, what's the difference between a solution and advice? Didn't the two sets of friends offer essentially the same feedback?

No.

A solution isn't necessarily characterized by a direct statement. For example, some men may, instead of using phrases like "What you should do is...." use an alternate phrasing of, "Well, what I would do in your place is...." This is still a "solution", because the phrasing is prescriptive. Whether the intro is "What you should do" or "What I would do" those and many other phrases still preface a solution; a description of how that other man would solve that problem. It's understood this is not offered to be bossy. It's a genuine expression of friendship. What is characteristic of all solutions is that they are *prescriptive* in that they direct the listener toward an action or outcome.

There is no issue when men offer solutions. You pick the best solution achieved through debate. Maybe you take part of a solution from this person and part from somewhere else, but the point is you find an answer.

Women tend not to offer solutions. It's inherently understood among females the best solution is the one the woman comes to of her own accord. Women assist by offering suggestions. Suggestions are not prescriptive. If we had to provide a word, we would say a suggestion is more descriptive; commonly offered as an interrogatory, that is, by asking thought provoking questions. You might be thinking, "Huh? What's the difference?"

Huge.

Notice the language women use. "Have you thought about this? Maybe it's time for that." Sure, women all over the world are just as capable of uttering "suggestions" the same way that men do, "You should just go in there and tell him off!" We're not saying that never happens. But even when it does, there would probably not be a defense of that plan. In female company, that's an exclamation of support. If the friend with the issue thinks that's a great idea, that could be discussed. If the friend doesn't pick up on it, it would likely be dropped very quickly.

While there are no "rules" about how men and women communicate, on average men offer "solutions" which are complete plans that they are willing to verbally defend until a solution is reached. Women offer "suggestions" which tend to be in the form of comments or questions intended to guide their friend towards a solution, but which would not be defended unless the friend verbally indicates another round is appropriate.

The problem occurs when you mix it up. Now let's go back to our male employee. His audience is his wife.

Wife: "That's terrible. I know how much you wanted a decent raise. Well, don't worry about it. We're surviving now, and we can keep surviving. Have you thought about talking to your boss?"

It could go either way, but we think this response, which among women would be excellent, would likely annoy most men. His wife is genuinely trying to be supportive. Ironically, most men would hear a metamessage in this statement as if she's condemning him for failing to get the raise. It's the opposite. She knows he wanted it. He didn't get it. She's reassuring him that there will be no pressure from her side. That's one less thing for him to worry about. The second thing that's annoying to a man is the suggestion. Not only did she not offer a solution which probably would have been fine, but he hasn't even offered his solution yet, and she's already questioning his ability to formulate one!

Now let's look at the reverse scenario. She comes home and reports the crummy raise to her husband.

Husband: "That sucks. You should go straight to HR. No, you shouldn't even have to go to HR. Maybe I should talk to this guy and let him know what I think of him giving my wife a crummy evaluation."

Now he's expressing his brand of support. He's offered two different solutions in one comment. Perfect! Even better, one solution involves considerable effort on his part. He should be getting major props for this, right?

Wrong.

She's probably super irritated. First, he's offered zero support. "That sucks" doesn't count. Then, he's given her two different solutions to this "problem", as if she's not intelligent enough to think up her own!

Wife: "Don't you dare. If I decide the best thing is to talk to my boss, I'll do it myself."

What this is intended to communicate is, "Back off. I can come up with my own solution." What he hears is, "I would like to hear you defend your solutions before I accept them."

Husband: "I know you're capable of talking to your boss. What I would do is go right to his office first thing tomorrow and get on his calendar. You don't want to wait until the paperwork is filed, and there's nothing he can do to change it." Support. Solution is reiterated and defended.

What she hears, "I'm saying I think you're capable of arriving at a solution, but it's clear I don't really believe you can because I'm continuing to offer my solution. For some mysterious reason, I have no desire to offer you any emotional support. I'm just offering a rational justification for why my solution is better."

It's going to devolve from there.

Your wife may be completely different than we're describing. If so, move on cheerfully to the next section. If you've had frustrating conversations like this where you felt you were sincerely offering her emotional support and she gave you feedback that she was annoyed, this is where the problem is coming from.

So here's what you can do. When your wife talks about a problem, any problem, don't immediately offer a solution. If you have trouble breaking this habit, try using a paraphrase first. A paraphrase is support because it simply re-articulates what the person already said. That's what women want when they ask for "support".

"Wow. Let me make sure I understand. Your boss gave you a bad evaluation which resulted in a crummy raise?" She may be happy with that response. You can say whatever you like if it communicates empathy. Empathy is anything that shows that you can "imagine" how the other person is feeling. Or if that doesn't work for you, "support" tends to include things that are happening now or in the past. It includes feelings not actions. So, "I'm so sorry your boss didn't appreciate you." "You must feel terrible about this. Let me hold you." But never, "I'll help you get over this."

Not Now! Maybe, Not Ever!

For men and women, we can broadly classify problems into two types: problems they want to solve, and problems they want to avoid. If someone indicates this is a problem they want to avoid, give up trying to help them immediately. No matter the outcome of your solution or support, if someone is determined to avoid a problem, it's unlikely to have a good outcome.

You will know they want to avoid the problem by how they respond. Men not only reject solutions. They will either overtly tell you to drop the subject, or they may propose ludicrous solutions. One of the authors tends to steer the conversation off into alien domination of the world as his verbal cue that he does not seriously wish to discuss a topic. Most people aren't quite that extreme, but probably not far off. While women may also use this technique, you can also watch for her to either overtly give you the message the discussion is over, or to give you a metamessage to that effect. An abrupt and drastic change of subject tends to signal that the person wishes to ... change the subject.

Ideally, you should avoid situations where your wife ends the conversation by not getting into them to begin with. If you listen attentively for her verbal cues and wait to offer advice until it's invited, then it's unlikely you will be in that situation.

Although your spouse might prefer otherwise, we recognize that in a marriage there may be problems that need to be solved. This is, perhaps, the trickiest situation you will face. Ironically, this is the only situation where you can propose a solution with impunity.

Suppose you have a financial crisis. You've just been laid off. Your credit cards are maxed. Something must be done immediately. You decide to refinance the debt into your mortgage. Your parents have agreed to co-sign, so your lack of employment is not an issue. You begin explaining this to your wife.

"The credit cards are a real problem right now...."

She interrupts with, "I don't want to hear another lecture on my spending."

She's receiving a metamessage you didn't intend to send, so you correct, "Honey, this isn't about your spending. It's about our debt."

"So? What do you expect me to do about it?"

This is a clear communication that she doesn't want to solve this problem, at least not now. However, we recommend you check in, attempt to re-engage her.

"I don't expect you to solve this problem. I think we need to discuss it. You probably don't want to talk about it right now, but unfortunately, it's a pressing matter."

"So, what do you think we should do about it?" The metamessage is to drop the subject. However, the subject cannot be dropped, and you have a clear invitation to provide a solution.

"I think we should refinance the debt into our mortgage. We can pay the mortgage with the income we have. My parents have agreed to co-sign."

"I don't like owing your parents. That's a crummy solution."

Try not to show emotion when your wife is being difficult. It tends to escalate the situation, providing an argument which is the change of topic she wants anyway.

"I respect your opinion. What would you suggest?"

"I don't have a suggestion. I don't want to talk about it right now."

At this point, you could ask her when she will be ready to provide a suggestion for a solution. If the problem allows you to delay, this is the best technique. Allowing her to pick a time when you will have the discussion forces her to commit to that discussion at that time. Then, if she still wants to avoid the issue, you're in a stronger position. If it does not, remain calm. Acknowledge her feelings but firmly continue the discussion.

"I completely understand that you don't want to talk about it. I can see how this upsets you." (Resist the urge to point out that you are also upset. That is not support from her perspective. That is a topic change, and she will want to switch to a subject she desires. This most likely will end up in an argument.) "I definitely would not pursue this any further," still acknowledging her feelings and professing your love, "but unfortunately this cannot wait."

"Well, I'm not going to talk about it tonight."

She's now told you five times that she refuses to cooperate to arrive at a solution. Check in and give her one final chance to participate.

"Unfortunately, this has to be resolved. If we delay, it will ruin our credit. I don't want to put you in that situation." Always phrase it as your problem. Your problem is you want to be the best husband you can be, and she won't let you do that. All completely true. "If we can't agree on an alternate solution, I'm going to contact the mortgage company tomorrow."

"I don't care. You're going to do what you want to do anyway."

A clear metamessage, but all you can do is bring the topic back up into overt language.

"I'm going to do what's best for both of us. I hope you'll think about it. If you have a different solution, I would love to hear it. I'll call tomorrow on my lunch break. If you come up with a different idea before then, please let me know." Profess your love. Make it clear you want to work with her, but give a definite deadline so there's no miscommunication. It wouldn't be a bad idea to check back one more time.

"Fine." Metamessage.

"Just to make sure I understand, you're going to think about this and let me know before noon if there's something else you want to do. If I don't hear from you, I will call the mortgage company."

She's going to be angry, but the anger is at the situation, not you - even if neither of you can appreciate that in the moment.

You gave her ample opportunity to revise her opinion and participate. You've checked in multiple times to allow her to disagree. At this point, your best bet is to offer support not with words, but with affection and let the discussion go. Her refusal to veto your solution constitutes acceptance. Please note, this is the ONLY situation where that is true. Reserve that for problem avoidance with multiple attempts to engage and check ins. If you abuse this, it will backfire. If you reserve this technique for catastrophic situations, there should be no issue. Presumably your wife is an adult and knows this is a serious situation. If you only push an issue when it must be pushed, she will most likely realize that you made every effort to include her and will probably be relieved when you execute your solution.

This is an exaggerated example. Most women will engage at some point. If this really happens, don't be bitter. We think it's unlikely someone would be this oppositional without good reason. Since her reaction is out of proportion to the situation, there is probably something in her past driving this response. When the crisis has passed, find a neutral time to raise the subject in a non-threatening manner.

"I wanted to talk about what happened with the credit card debt. I felt really bad that you couldn't help me come up with a plan to resolve the issue." Keep it about your feelings. It's not about her behavior. If you criticize her behavior, you will just alienate her and not achieve anything. "You seemed really upset. I know there's a good chance we will have issues like this in the future, and I would like to understand why you reacted that way and what I can do better in the future."

Some reader is shaking his head and thinking, "Why can't I call her on her behavior? She acted like a child!"

You can do whatever you want. It's our job to give you the best options. With a reaction this intense, something is driving her response. Absolutely, the problem is on her side in this exact scenario. Would you rather be right, or would you rather be married?

Criticizing her behavior is not going to make her feel safe enough to give you the information you're seeking. Negative reactions come out of negative experiences. At a base level, all negative experiences stem from a violation of trust. Think of every negative experience you've had. If it wasn't just a horrible

112

event like a car accident, then it was a situation where you had certain expectations, and someone did something contrary to those expectations. That's a violation of trust. Even with an event like a car accident, it's still a trust violation. You expected to be able to control the vehicle, or the driver would control the vehicle, and didn't. From then on, you won't trust riding in a vehicle for a while. One of the authors lost a parent in a car accident when he was a teenager. Not only did this cause an issue with riding in cars and planes, it also made abandonment a hot button. In our teen years, unless there are extenuating circumstances, we expect our parents to be there. This "betrayal" of that "trust" gives rise to anxiety. Who else that "promised" to be there will disappear without notice? How do you depend on someone to keep their word when life might prevent them from doing so?

So, it's likely this type of reaction is coming out of a serious betrayal of trust. If you don't already know what caused it, you must provide a "safe" place for your wife to discuss it. If she trusts that your love is unconditional then she's more likely to open up. By NOT criticizing her you are deliberately sending a metamessage that it's all right for her to express her feelings. She can decode that message. If she doesn't want to talk about it then, shelve it and return to the topic periodically in non-threatening circumstances. Eventually, she will feel comfortable confiding in you.

Family Values

Problem-solving in a marriage is also going to be affected by your value system. In every partnership, there is some division of labor. Some problems will be yours to solve and you don't need to work with your spouse. For example, let's say you do all the cooking. What to buy for groceries and what to cook each night are your problems exclusively.

When the problem belongs to you exclusively, you do not generally have to check in with your partner. However, you should proactively work to manage her expectations by keeping her appraised of your solutions. "Honey, I thought we would have steak on Friday. How does that sound to you?"

Problems that exclusively belong to her are hers to solve. You do, however, have the right to be appraised of the solution. Further, your interest in her solution counts as romance. "Honey,

I know you were planning to go to the dentist. Did you make the appointment? When is it?"

It's important to negotiate who will be in charge of which problems. Don't assume you know the answer. Perhaps you grew up in a traditional household where your mother cooked all meals. You see your marriage as traditional as well. Don't automatically expect her to do all the cooking. Even if you failed to negotiate years ago, it's never too late to clarify. "You know, I love the way you cook. But it occurs to me, I never asked you if you wanted to do the cooking. I just assumed you would. Are you happy with this arrangement?"

Even if you don't seek or couldn't accommodate a change, still open the topic, negotiate, and arrive at a mutually agreeable solution.

"Well, no, it's not actually. I've been doing all the cooking for ten years and I hate cooking."

"I'm sorry to hear that. I apologize for never having asked. As you know, I have trouble toasting bread. It's unlikely we would be happy if I started cooking. But maybe you could teach me, and I could eventually take over one meal a week."

Even if you end up with the status quo, she will appreciate the fact that you asked.

Teamwork Means Working *with* The Team

Ideally, when solving mutual problems, you will work as a team. When working as a team, make sure you give her space to really be part of the team. If you're a natural leader, don't always take the lead. That's not equal. Conversely, if you hate leading, don't always try to get her to run the show. She may be sick of that too.

But the most important aspect of teamwork is communication. If you're still struggling with that, please reread the preceding chapters.

If a problem comes down to two solutions that are mutually exclusive, be sure to pick your battles. Weigh the benefit of getting your way against the toll it might take in your marriage. Use active listening to ensure you arrive at a mutually agreeable solution.

114

Most issues where two parties are in opposition can be resolved by a compromise. A compromise is where you give up part of what you want as the solution. If you're not giving up something, but not all, of your solution, or if she is not getting something, if not all, of what she wants, then it's not a compromise.

If a problem belongs exclusively to her, do not offer a solution unless solicited. Even then, tread lightly. Even if you think she has a disastrous solution, it's her learning experience. You can't save your wife from every mistake she could ever make. Mistakes are experiments through which humans mature. They're her mistakes to make. However, if you truly believe she's making a huge mistake with dire consequences, all you can do is offer empathy and support. Act as her most trusted advisor because that is your position. Ask questions to help her take a second look at the situation. Be open to having your mind changed. It might be you will "learn" that her solution isn't the wrong solution. It's just not the same as yours. Remember, she's probably not sharing her concerns so you can "fix" them. Wait for her to ask for your opinion before you offer it.

The take-aways from this chapter are:

1. Stereotypically, men provide solutions to each other. Women provide support and suggestions.

2. Don't offer a solution to one of your wife's problems without being invited to do so. Do offer your wife support and advice when she needs it. Do offer a solution if specifically requested to provide one.

3. Some people on certain issues aren't problem-solvers, they're problem avoiders.

4. If your wife is avoiding an issue, make multiple overtures to get her to work with you on that issue. If that doesn't work, try harder. As a last resort, you can provide and implement a solution if she invites you to do or if the problem is so urgent you don't have time/money to negotiate a solution at a pace with which she's comfortable.

5. Values may govern how things are done in the marriage but it's good to negotiate who will own which problems.

6. If a problem is exclusively yours, manage expectations by keeping her appraised of your solutions; expect and request the same courtesy from her.

Chapter Thirteen

Would You Like A Grudge With That?

Now that we've talked about problem solving, we just want to spend some time addressing the lack thereof which can become a huge issue if not addressed.

At the risk of being over-stereotypical, problems tend to be resolved for men when the problem itself ends. Problems tend to be resolved for women when they make emotional peace with the situation. Another important difference between the two genders is how they get over problems after they're resolved. Men tend to put problems behind them by getting distance in terms of time. Women, if they put the problem behind them, do not need distance per se. However, since it is so much more difficult for them to get resolution, it may seem like they just never get over the issue.

It's The End Of Our World As We Know It

The types of problems we're interested in here are interpersonal; it doesn't have to be big problems like infidelity, but we are talking about problems that affect emotions. That is not to say that what we're going to talk about would never be true if let's say your bank messes up the mortgage. But let's face it, your wife holding a grudge against the mortgage company is not why you bought this book.

Let's say you and your wife have a disagreement on the night of your annual *something* party and she doesn't go. You're angry. There's a fight. She apologizes. End of story.

What are the odds you're going to bring that up in the future?

Sure, it could happen, but we don't think it's very likely. There has been damage to trust. If there is no further behavior like this on her part, then we think the husband is most likely to put it behind him. When it's brought up, then it's irritating all over again. If it's never brought up again, it's not irritating any more.

Once the problem is over, after all, you can't go back in time to the event she missed, and she apologized. That's the end of the discussion.

That doesn't mean you don't continue to feel hurt. It doesn't mean you don't have any long-term effects. All we're saying is that we think the more long-term the effects, the less you will want to rehash it because we believe that men tend to need distance to recover emotionally.

When there's a long-term negative emotional reaction to a circumstance, we would call that a "grudge." This negative feeling becomes like a boat anchor dragging behind the relationship, slowing it down. Each separate grudge is probably treated like a separate anchor.

For want of a better metaphor, men deal with grudges by putting time between themselves and the incident. The metaphoric "rope" holding the anchor stretches thin until it simply breaks and the grudge goes away. At that point, men are usually amenable to talking about the incident again. The distance is such that it's just another story.

Women do not work like that.

Let's reverse the situation. He doesn't attend her annual something. There's a fight. He apologizes.

We're nowhere near the end of the event and its resolution.

Is Love Never Having To Say, 'I'm Sorry'?

First, how you apologize to your wife makes a huge difference. We only touched on apologies in earlier chapters.

When apologizing to your wife, you must first decide if (objectively) you were in the wrong. For most people, an apology is an admission of guilt. If you were, accept ownership of that during your apology. "I'm sorry I boycotted your annual something. I was in the wrong. I'm truly sorry for that."

118

Regardless of whether the incident is something that will never repeat, or that repeats multiple times per day, by definition, an apology concerns an event that is in the past.

If you were truly not in the wrong, then you apologize for the way it made her feel. "I'm sorry I made you unhappy by skipping your annual something. It pains me to know I made you feel unhappy and I'm truly sorry for that."

Those are two completely different apologies. Think carefully before you give the second one. Many women won't pick up the difference. But if your wife does, you have to be ready to address that.

When apologizing to another man, this is typically the end. Sometimes it will go one more round where your friend might say, "Yeah, you were in the wrong! You made me look like an idiot!"

"I know, and I'm really sorry."

End of story.

When apologizing to a woman, go right into the next phase. There is no need to check in until the apology is made.

Now *That's* An Apology

For women, an affective apology, at minimum, will include the following:

1. Admission of responsibility: either true guilt or responsibility for the effect of your actions.

2. Acknowledgement of how your actions made her feel and the root cause of that feeling. (Address the social aspect, tone, body language, as appropriate.)

3. Acknowledgement that any apology is inadequate with a sincere request for forgiveness.

4. Promise to not repeat the behavior.

5. Expression of emotional support.

Remember, women process communication on multiple levels. Men generally don't. Your apology must clearly show you're aware of what your actions truly meant to her. Otherwise, the perception is that this is just a "guy" apology on a "guy" level. If you think about this, we think you will see this as "fair." If she's the injured party, she deserves an apology that meets her criteria. If you are worried that you have not thought up all the ramifications of the act from her perspective, ask her or at least listen to what she says about what happened. Most likely she will list some that you didn't think about, and you can incorporate those into your apology. Most likely you will have to listen to her vent even before you can apologize. Be attentive. Don't waste this valuable opportunity for insight into why she's angry and hurt.

So, a true apology might look something like this:

"(1) I'm sorry I boycotted your annual something. I was in the wrong and I'm truly sorry for that. (2) I realize that when we argued about whatever, we were both very angry. But I should not have skipped your annual something. This is your one chance per year to do something, and I feel bad that you probably couldn't enjoy it because I didn't attend. It must have been very difficult and possibly humiliating for you to have to answer questions about why I wasn't there. I put you in the terrible position of being caught between lying to your friends to cover for my bad behavior or admitting the issue and airing our dirty laundry in public. I'm your husband and no matter what arguments we have, that is no excuse for being derelict in my duties. (3) I realize now that I could have and should have handled this differently. It wasn't fair of me to use your annual else something to punish you for something that was completely unrelated. I know that nothing I say can erase this from your heart and your mind. You may be dealing with this for a while. I'm genuinely sorry for that. Even though this will take a while for you to get over, I hope you can find it in your heart to truly forgive me. (4) If I could go back and change it, I would. I know that must sound empty. All I can really do is honestly promise you that this will never happen again. Not only will I not spoil your annual something in future, I will also never use a public function as a weapon against you. (5) I love you so much, Honey. I'm so sorry I screwed up. I'll do whatever I can to support you through this."

Now that's an apology.

There probably will be three to six rounds after this where she expresses her feelings or chews you out. Listen attentively. Don't get defensive. Reiterate the main points of your apology as necessary. When she seems to be winding down, or if she starts crying, etc. then hold her.

Know this issue may resurface from time to time. If your apology was sincere, it shouldn't be problematic to repeat it.

She cannot move on until she feels you truly understand the magnitude of what this meant to her life. When similar circumstances arise in future, she will be watching your behavior. Your actions, whether you repeat the behavior or not, will tell her if your apology was sincere. If it was not, marriages can only take so many of these grudges before they collapse. A man wants time so that the anchor of a grudge grows thin and breaks. Women handle this differently. They are constantly re-evaluating that anchor. Should it be wrapped in more grudges until it becomes so heavy the marriage drowns? Or, should it get lighter and lighter until the drag is negligent, and it just disappears? When she brings the issue up, she can either make the anchor lighter or heavier. If you're defensive; unapologetic; "this again?" - all those reactions send the metamessage that in the moment you snowed her. She must trust that you were genuine, and that trust is built by your being dependable and predictable. No doubt this will irritate you. You're trying to get away from that anchor. She keeps hauling it in close to the boat.

If it's gone, does it matter how it disappeared?

But I Really *Didn't* Do Anything Wrong

If you genuinely (objectively) feel you did nothing wrong, the apology looks slightly different; and you must be willing to back that up. So really think before you go this route. Is it worth it?

If it is, the elements will be (changes in bold):

1. Admission of responsibility: either true guilt or responsibility for the effect of your actions.

2. Acknowledgement of how your actions made her feel and the root cause of that feeling. (Address the social aspect, tone, body language, as appropriate.)

3. **Optional explanation of why you acted as you did (motive must be pro-relationship).**

4. Acknowledgement that any apology is inadequate with a sincere request for forgiveness.

5. Promise to not repeat the behavior.

6. Expression of emotional support.

Remember, your "reason" needs to relate to something positive about your marriage or just go with option one. If your reason doesn't also benefit her, your actions were selfish; and you can't choose option two. Selfish actions in the context of a marriage are not morally right. You need to (more objectively) re-evaluate the situation.

Please understand, we're fudging this example. In the scenario we've set up, it's unlikely the husband was in the right. But for the sake of example, that apology would look more like this (changes in bold):

"(1) **I'm sorry I made you feel unhappy by skipping your annual something. It pains me to know that I made you unhappy, and I'm truly sorry for that.** (2) I realize that when we argued about whatever, we were both very angry. But I should not have skipped your annual something. This is your one chance per year to do something, and I feel bad that you probably couldn't enjoy it because I didn't attend. It must have been very difficult and possibly humiliating for you to have to answer questions about why I wasn't there. **I understand you feel like** I put you in the terrible position of being caught between lying to your friends to cover for my bad behavior or admitting the issue and airing our dirty laundry in public. I'm your husband and no matter what arguments we have, that is no excuse for being derelict in my duties. (3) **At the time, it felt like the right thing to do. We were arguing about how I always get drunk and embarrass you. I know that I could** have not had a drink or, in the worst case scenario, I could have called my sponsor. But I thought about how much you want me to put drinking behind me. The potential to ruin all the hard work we've put into helping me recover seemed so great, I just thought the best thing for us long-term as a couple would be to just skip it. I didn't think you would care. I figured you would rather just have me not show up than call you when you were so angry. So, instead of attending your annual something, I went to a meeting instead.** (4) I realize now that I could have and should have handled this differently. It wasn't fair of me to **act in a way that made you feel like I was** using your annual something to punish you for something else that was completely unrelated. I know that nothing I say can erase this from your heart and your mind. You may be dealing with this for a while. I'm genuinely sorry for that. Even though this will take a while for you to get over, I hope you can find it in your heart to truly forgive me. (5) If I could go back and change it, I would. I know that must sound empty. All I can really do is honestly promise you that this will never happen again. Not only will I not spoil your annual something in future, I will also never **do anything that would make you feel like I was** using a public function as a weapon against you. (6) I love you so much, Honey. I'm so sorry I screwed up. I'll do whatever I can to support you through this."

If you think this is a bit much, that the husband is in the right due to his reason, reread. Then ask yourself: do you really believe there is any justifiable reason for purposely acting in a way that makes your wife feel bad?

If the answer is yes, you need to seriously consider if you're abusive towards her. If that's the case, get help immediately.

We think abusive partners "love" their spouses, sometimes as much as non-abusive. The difference is they believe that if there is an acceptable excuse, behavior that hurts their spouse is acceptable. Justified. It is never ok to hurt your spouse or for her to hurt you. Period. So if your actions hurt her, you should be able to apologize for that.

The Never-Ending Grudge

Many men might be thinking, "Ok, but how long do I let this go on? My wife has been bringing the same stuff up for years. I can't take it anymore!"

First, honestly assess whether you've given an adequate apology. If she's still bringing it up, is it because you've never given her resolution?

From your perspective, if you have given her resolution, then you must discuss this with her.

Pick a neutral time to have the discussion. Bubble bath with fancy wine maybe? When you open the discussion, you need to be careful with what you say. This is one situation where you really don't want this to end up in an argument because that's going to be like lead plating on that anchor.

During this discussion, you need to try to keep everything calm enough to make three points:

1. This is obviously still bothering her, so why? IE: what can you do to finally satisfy her on this issue?

2. You are willing to do whatever she says she needs (and you MUST do that after the conversation is over).

3. You want a firm commitment from her that if you do what she asks, she will give you a clean slate. Period. No more revisiting this issue. It's over.

Remember to make this about you and your feelings. Try to send her the right metamessages. Don't criticize her behavior. You are mentally *completely* willing to just give her all the time she needs but you're emotionally too fragile to do that.

Do you feel offended? Don't be. If you're having this conversation, that's the absolute truth. If that truth makes you comfortable, don't have the conversation. We're not all women working on this book, and no man on this team is a stranger to having to swallow his pride. We don't want to sugar coat anything too much.

If you treat every issue in your marriage like it might be the last straw, then you will always be prepared to prevent that last straw from being added to the burden. In our marriages, we would rather be too serious and be pleasantly surprised, than not take something serious that is and lose the marriage because of that.

A conversation to negotiate a fresh start would go something like this:

"A few years (decade) ago, we had an argument and I didn't go to your annual something with you. At the time, I apologized, and I feel like I've done my best to make it up to you and show you that my apology was sincere. And yet, every year you bring it back up. Clearly this is still a sore spot for you. I know I hurt you at the time, but I don't understand why the hurt is still so fresh. Can you help me to understand?"

Now you listen with every active listening skill you've got. If she explains this to you, it's probably going to answer a ton of other questions. In the best of circumstances, this will take the two of you off on an intimate bonding journey long overdue that will be worth that decade of annoyance. As she explains, be supportive. Hold her. Don't interrupt her. If she falters, be supportive. Empathize and ask her questions to help her articulate the issue. Women can be just as rough as men. Maybe she doesn't know why. Maybe she's going to be sorry she's been hurting you. This is your marriage, do what feels right.

If there's no chick flick moment, don't be discouraged. Maybe next time. If she just justifies the behavior or berates you or whatever, listen carefully. Mentally take notes. Then move on to part two.

"Let me make sure I understand you. You just can't move on because the women in your group keep heckling you. I totally understand. But this really hurts me because it reminds me of a time when I screwed up. What can I do to finally deserve a clean slate?"

Again, listen. Take notes. Be willing to do those things. Then move on to part three.

"Let me make sure I understand you. You need me to apologize to you in front of the women in your group and stand on my head for ten minutes. If I do that, can you really forgive me? This is so upsetting to me, as difficult as this would be for do, I'm willing to do it. But if you can't forgive me after that, it will just destroy me emotionally. I have to know that if I do this you can really let go of this part of our past so we can move forward into a more loving relationship."

If she agrees, do it. To the letter. No matter how dumb, humiliating, whatever. Unless your spouse is abusive, she's not doing this for retribution. This is what she really needs from

125

you. Be a good enough husband to meet her needs. That's what you agreed to when you got married.

If for some reason, she doesn't keep her part of the bargain, then you are truly, finally in the right on this issue. You can then calmly but firmly remind her of the agreement and request she keep her side of the bargain. Again, unless she's abusive, she will.

Grudges, if not addressed, can really quickly kill a marriage on either side. If you're in the wrong, give her the benefit of the doubt. Work with her. But also protect yourself. Just as we're advising you to put the marriage ahead of your own needs, we would advise her the same. One party alone cannot solve these issues. She must be willing to let go of the grudge to get the much better prize of a healthy relationship.

The take-aways from this chapter are:

1. Grudges become anchors that weigh down the relationship.

2. Men get over grudges by getting distance from the incident; women get over grudges by revisiting them until they feel the issue is resolved.

3. To help your wife achieve resolution, make a full and complete apology (see above) for the act or how the act made her feel.

4. Only apologize for her hurt feelings if your "reason" for committing the act was for the benefit of the relationship. If you can't explain this properly, you don't have a good "reason" and you should apologize for the act itself.

5. Be prepared and patient if she raises the issue multiple times.

6. If you are SURE you have made a good apology and she won't let it go, negotiate an act or acts of contrition to achieve a "clean slate."

7. Perform the acts of contrition to the letter (and spirit) of the agreement.

Chapter Fourteen

Do You Still Have A Headache?

"All he wants to do is have sex."
"He should want to be making love."
"Get real. How many guys 'make love'?"

If you jumped right to this chapter, stop. Go back. The reason this chapter is at the end is not to just keep you reading for the whole book. It's because you need all the other information first.

It's an old truism that women fall in love and then want to have sex; men have sex and then fall in love. We're fully aware there are plenty of people who don't work like this either because they just don't or because their value systems prohibit sex outside of marriage. But there's a reason for the old jump rope rhyme, "First comes love, then comes marriage, then comes someone in the baby carriage." Kids might not grasp the implication, but as adults we know that between marriage and the baby carriage came sex.

Even if you don't believe you work like this, it is true of many people. This is why porn tends to be more effective for men. Stereotypically, usually just the offer of sex is enough to get a man's interest. His wife says, "Are you in the mood?" If he wasn't, he is now! He says, "Are you in the mood?" She either already was or probably won't be. Of course, maybe he can change her mind. But how would he do that?

For many people, Romance=Sex because romance is (stereotypically) what puts a woman in the mood. The psychological predates the physical.

This is not a how-to book on sex acts. We will provide some concrete advice towards the end, but it was never intended to be a guide to the variety and efficacy of various sex acts. If that's what you're seeking, there are plenty of great books out there. Or, send us a message; maybe we'll write one. But this isn't it. We presume our readers know all about the mechanics of sex. If not, that's a totally different issue.

But no book on marriage would be complete without addressing the issue of sex so we'll do our best.

When couples disagree on sex, it's generally either about the frequency or the quality. If one partner wants more frequent physical intimacy than the other, first you need to figure out (as a couple) if it's disinterest or an inability to perform. Certain physical and mental health conditions, medications, not to mention age, work to change a person's sex drive. If your spouse is having difficulty with a physical issue, no book in the world can fix that. Go see a physician. That's the best we can do.

If it's disinterest, that's a different story.

At the risk of over-generalizing, we think most men probably want less sex if there are quasi-physical issues. Maybe he's too tired to "make it." If your wife complains you aren't in the mood enough, maybe there's something going on with you physically that is contributing to that condition. Maybe not a classic cause like low testosterone but just not enough sleep or too much stress.

If your issue is that you just don't find your wife attractive enough anymore, we have no advice for you. There's no good advice to give. We feel love is what drives marriage (ok, we're old fashioned). When you got married, you could have reasonable been expected to look ahead and realize that if marriage is supposed to be "Until death do us part," this could plausibly be expected to include old age. It doesn't sound like you got married for the right reasons.

We hope most of our readers would not have this issue - our book is written for those who want to revitalize their marriage. But let it not be said that we didn't address a logical possibility.

If you're just not in the mood, is it psychological? Just because most men's sex drives are not related to their emotional state doesn't mean yours isn't. Maybe you just don't feel intimate with your partner emotionally. In that case, we hope that this book has begun to resolve those issues. Try discussing what you've learned with her. Find out what she considers to be a positive change in the relationship and ask her to also make a positive change toward how she relates to you. We're not invested in being "right" about how each gender functions. Hopefully the whole book can be the basis of many fun discussions. Maybe she will discover some things that she didn't realize was going on and work on the relationship too. That could really have a positive effect on your sex-drive.

Women have just as active sex drives as men. If you continually turn your wife down when she seeks physical intimacy or if you treat it as a chore, she will probably feel rejected. Particularly as someone ages, sexual desirability may stand in as a barometer for how well one is aging. We find it hard to believe that anyone in 2020 would not be aware that many women are treated by society as sexual objects. For any woman not your wife, that's not ok. But your wife expects that from you. Even if a physical problem prevents you from performing, take extra care to make sure she knows that if it was up to you, you would take her up on it in a heartbeat. Meanwhile, investigate alternative resolutions. Is there something you two can try that would be extra exciting?

If your wife is not open to having as much sex as you would like, it's possible it's a quasi-physical cause like lack of sleep. But we would tend to suspect that it's a lack of emotional intimacy.

Women tend to need more foreplay than men. For most women, foreplay starts when you greet her in the morning and continues with every interaction thereafter. Why do romantic movies show the couple engaged in some cute "couple-y" behavior before a sex scene? Well, because that puts her in the mood.

That's why all the chapters before this were so important. If you know Romance=Attention, you can manage expectations. You have worked hard to develop trust. You've improved your style of communication - your frequency, type, content, is satisfying to her. You're decoding and responding well to metamessages, not to mention the fact that your actions, your approach to problem-solving and your grudge resolution techniques are all off the chart. If you've done all that, we think there's a good chance she's in the mood a lot more often now than she was before you started.

Still, if that's not working, why not just talk to her? Find out what more she needs. Maybe it's something straightforward and easily resolved. Maybe it's not, but you can still work on it together. Maybe she just needs your attention to feel special. Is there anything you can try to spice up your sex lives that might really engage her?

Remember, Romance=Attention. Even if she has trouble getting into the mood, if you organize a full frontal ... wait for it, romantic encounter, does that help? You wake her up with breakfast in bed, poem on the tray professing your love and go from there, does that make a difference? If it does, keep working the previous chapters. As you begin to make the marriage stronger, it probably won't take a super-husband effort to stoke her fire.

If her issue is not being attracted to you enough, we're sorry to hear that. We hope you will tell her the same thing we just told you. This is not out of left field to think that within the context of a marriage someone's body type can change.

Regardless of on which side, if this happens, you can't go back in time and unmarry. You have already wasted (presumably) a lot of each other's time. Be honest but not mean about the issue and come up with a resolution. You are married now: will you continue? If so, the partner with the issue is going to have to try to get over it. It's one thing to deny your partner intimacy if there 's a legitimate physical disability. It's another to give them the cold shoulder because you want someone else on a physical level.

While couples do exist for whom an open relationship works, we highly recommend you think carefully as a couple before opening that door. Once it's open, it can't be closed. Unless you had an agreement before marriage, presumably you both signed on for fidelity. Besides the tax benefits, that's a big part of what marriage "means." It's a contract for life. Once signed, you usually can't rewrite a contract without major penalties.

Some people are totally fine in relationships with no sex. If that's the case, then there's no issue. If not, it's a big issue. By its institution, marriage might imply that you're only having sex with your spouse, but it certainly implies you're having sex. If one of you says they're fine with having a platonic marriage, the other better do a whole lot of checking in for the rest of the marriage. Maybe they're fine now, but that could easily change. Maybe they just want to please you; but when the reality of a sexless marriage sets in, that doesn't feel as acceptable. You each have but one life to live. Formally ending the chance/hope/expectation of sex is a huge bait and switch. Whichever side is doing that, you both need to be super honest about your feelings. If you're not, you're just throwing good time after bad.

If you or she is just a super visual or tactile person, can you both work together to change the circumstances? Nothing is going to reverse aging. Even late in life, it is possible to get to a gym and tone up. Is this something you can do together?

Remember, in this circumstance, the "disgruntled" partner has the onus on them to be the leader in developing a solution. If your wife thinks you're too flabby to sleep with, then she has to say what she needs to fix that. "It can't be fixed" is not acceptable. And the same is true if the issue is reversed. Otherwise, you both need to sit down and decide if this is a deal-breaker and go from there. Unfortunately, there are some issues a book can't resolve. But we don't really have any more sympathy for a woman who allows physical beauty or lack thereof to control their sex drive than we would for a man.

Moving on.

Since the desire for more/less sex can be from either side, we won't differentiate too much more based on gender. The solution to most issues in the bedroom is communication. Depending on age or gender, this may be difficult. If you or your spouse has been raised to see talking about sex as taboo, start slow. But start. If you don't talk about the issues, they can't get resolved.

Maybe you or she wants to try something new, and the other party is not open to that. Maybe they really aren't open or maybe they just need to know why you're interested in it. Some things just won't work for some people. Other people can do anything once if it means pleasing their partner. Maybe if you try it, the reluctant party will discover they love it. Maybe the eager party will find out it's a let-down. Many people covet experiences that are "forbidden." When that's no longer the case, interest fades. But the discussion could reveal alternatives, or just feeling loved enough to be accommodated might change their perspective and beef up their sex-drive.

Maybe the issue is that after orgasm, one party always falls asleep. That's a common effect. Regardless of which party has the issue, talk about it. There's nothing wrong with saying, "Honey, after we make love, you always fall asleep. It makes me feel like you're just using me for my body. I know you don't mean it this way," (always give your spouse the benefit of the doubt), "but that's how I feel. Is there any way to resolve this?" Maybe you're the sleeping lover. You can always say, "Let me make sure I understand. You feel objectified when I fall asleep after sex. But I just can't help it. Could you perhaps let me take a ten-minute power nap and then wake me up?" Problem solved. Or maybe you're choosing the wrong time to be intimate. Many couples, due to time constraints or privacy constraints, wait until late at night to have sex. Is there a way to change the schedule?

There's a reason many films and books show "pillow talk." Post-coital conversation is a great time to follow up physical intimacy with emotional intimacy. Some people need that. Others don't. Maybe your relationship is so awesome you have great bonding all day long and you both want to crash after sex. If you find out what she needs and you let her know what you need, you can manage expectations and have a much better sex life.

Few issues are as emotionally charged as sex. If there's a mismatch in your desires and expectations, that can snowball fast. The only way to resolve this issue is to work through it like any other "problem." Ignoring it is never going to make it go away.

Whether you believe in Darwinism or Adam and Eve, most people agree there's a biological imperative to procreate that doesn't necessarily just go away when you're done having children or if you never choose to have any. For most issues, if there's a mismatch, you just have better communication and work it out. Different needs regarding sex isn't a difference of opinion: it's biology. It's not like you wanted red curtains and she wanted blue. It's more like one spouse needs a different amount of oxygen in their atmosphere. Sure, some people can adapt to low or high altitude. Some people get sick.

All our research indicates that sexuality is formed early in life. That doesn't mean it can't morph over time. When we say "morph" we don't mean "change drastically", like you thought you were gay and got into a straight marriage hoping you'd grow out of it. More like you were never really into oral sex, then you

132

discovered you like it. Maybe something has changed on one or both sides since you got married. Or, maybe you either didn't discuss sex before marriage (thinking it will take care of itself) or you weren't honest with each other at that time. Either way, it's not fair to ask your spouse to change who they are, especially since not everyone can.

Be honest with each other. Try to resolve the issue. If you can't, admit that and stop wasting each other's time.

What you MUST not do is lie to your spouse and say you're ok with the resolution and then seek satisfaction outside of the marriage. You are at the end of a book filled with examples of why, even if it weren't immoral, it won't work. We hope that you can see for yourself this "solution" is just putting off an inevitable breakup. The same is true of her and you should emphasize that the only thing more important to you than how she feels about your marriage, if anything, is her honest expression of those feelings.

You're Doing It Wrong

There are all sorts of reasons why one or both partners may feel a sexual encounter was "bad." But most of them shouldn't put a strain on your relationship. Of course, if your spouse calls out someone else's name during sex, that's "bad." But that kind of issue is well beyond the scope of this work.

When we say "bad" sex what we mean is "unsatisfying sex". While sex can be satisfying without an orgasm, if you assume it's not, you probably won't ever hear your wife argue with that assumption.

Additionally, factors that prevent orgasm which are outside of the control of the participants, usually do not strain the marriage. If you're having sex and your infant wakes up and one partner goes to tend to the baby, you might both be bummed but it's irrational to blame either parent.

So, we are defining "bad" sex as one or both partners failing to achieve orgasm as a result of the action or inaction of the other.

There's no way to sugar coat this: guys, we're talking about you.

It should be no secret that the male sex organ is not difficult to locate. Female genetalia can be a little more elusive. We think it's probably rare for guys not to "cross the finish line" once they start the race unless the entire act is interrupted, or he suffers an episode of impotence. For women, on the other hand, achieving orgasm is more like trying to get through a symphony orchestra. There are a lot of individual inputs any of which can delay or derail the entire performance. Unfortunately, that's just biology.

Just because it's harder for her to achieve orgasm doesn't mean it's impossible. If your partner doesn't climax occasionally, it is what it is. If this is a regular occurrence, and she's not as interested in sex as you are, that could be why. Further, this can be a source of frustration that not only inhibits interest but can also lead to grudges, bitterness, and worse.

For most women, sex starts with foreplay and ends with affection. An orgasm will occur somewhere towards the end of this cycle, but it is not the actual end.

Some people become really upset if there is no post-orgasmic activity. "Making love" is about more than just intercourse, ejaculation and passing out. Many men may find that timeline perfectly wonderful, and there's no value judgement here if you fall into that category. But, understand that most women don't.

Just as women communicate with more than just the overt meaning of the words being exchanged, they make love with the totality of their being as well. We were quite serious when we said foreplay starts when she gets up in the morning. It runs throughout the day through the orgasm right into the post-orgasm cuddling and conversation. Not all women want conversation, and not all women who do want it every time. But we feel safe stating that the vast majority of, if not all, women want cuddling and affection afterwards. If you don't provide post-orgasm support, the perception is that you are simply "having sex" not "making love." If she doesn't climax, the perception is, right or wrong, that it's your "fault" and you're selfish and uncaring. The more that perception is reinforced, the more likely she will either want less sex, less marriage, or less of both.

The language provides incredible insight into how women perceive physical intimacy. We "have" sex, but we "make" love. The latter is more than just a euphemism (alternate way) of referring to the act of sex.

When you "have" something you can "possess" it ("I have a car") or you can "consume" it ("Every morning, I have breakfast."). The dictionary provides an additional meaning of, "To experience or undergo" as in "to have a good time."

While it's plausible this last definition might be what's intended ("Are we having fun yet? Yes, we're having sex."), we shouldn't discount the other meanings. It's unlikely this is **not** meant as a double (or triple) entendre.

By contrast, we "make" love. "Make" means "to form something" or to "cause it to come into being or existence." The metamessage is that the sexual act is a creative endeavor, which, to be fair, for women it sometimes is exactly that.

It's not surprising that women are more interested in the (pro) creative aspect; they are, after all, the ones who will give birth to the baby if conception occurs. But "love" probably isn't a careless choice either. As a noun, "love" means "an intense feeling of deep affection" or "a great interest and pleasure in something." As a verb, the definition is "to feel a deep romantic or sexual attachment to" something.

There's nothing inherently physical about love. It's a purely emotional concept. What this means is that someone who values "making love" is more interested in the emotional aspect than the physical. And, while women may or may not require an emotional attachment prior to the physical act of sex, the result should be the creation of an even deeper emotional attachment after consummation.

In the context of a marriage, it requires both parties to collaborate in order to create this resultant love. A woman can no more unilaterally decide to "make love" than she can unilaterally decide to procreate a child. We know this is true, because no native English speaker would use the phrase "make love" to describe a solitary act like masturbation.

So, when women talk about "making love", they are saying in effect is that the physical act of sex has a critical emotional component jointly created by both partners. Men who "have sex" are, from a woman's perspective, in a very real way, doing it wrong. It shouldn't be difficult then to understand why the failure of a partner to address this emotional aspect can engender scorn and derision. Even if he only requires a physical act (which may or may not be true but is certainly more typical for men than women), she requires an emotional component. His failure to contribute his part to that (mutual) creation of emotion must be a priori a selfish and uncaring action. Therefore, having sex is literally the antithesis of making love. That certainly justifies quite a bit of what is perceived as well-deserved criticism and scorn.

This might be too long of an explanation of the situation for you. In that case, just accept that to your wife the support and affection after the sexual activity ends is just as, if not more, important than the act itself. No matter how good your performance, if you routinely fail to provide support and affection afterwards, it may not "count" as making love. Couple this with your wife not climaxing (notice the word climax: "the most intense, exciting, or important point of something; a culmination or apex." What goes up should come down), and this is almost certainly the case.

(Note: though we set out with a dedication to be as clinical and PG as possible, we feel we would be failing from an educational perspective if we didn't provide some biological information. If you are not of age or if this subject offends you, then skip to the take-always. We will provide practical information as well but you're going to have to be patient. Where we provide citations, our conclusions are the result of online research. Everything else is the result of practical experience. While the basis of these are not in formal science, that should not be construed as a lack of disciplined observation.)

You Come and Go

So, if the wife doesn't have an orgasm, does this mean that the husband is in fact a selfish prick?

This may not be the case. Aside from the fact that some women may fake an orgasm for a number of reasons, there are also some really-easy-to-understand-non-duplicitous explanations as to why, if your wife doesn't have an orgasm, it's not because you're selfish or why you might not be able to tell if she climaxed or not.

First, besides the obvious differences between the genetalia in each gender, there are also very real differences in how the body functions during sex.

Remember when you went through puberty? Hormones are powerful stuff!

From a strictly biological perspective, conception doesn't happen unless a spermatozoon fertilizes an egg. Based on nothing more than common sense, we suggest this is the underlying cause of premature ejaculation.

Men seem "hardwired" to achieve arousal and then ejaculation at a fast rate. Certainly, much faster than women.

From a purely biological perspective, that women are slower makes sense as well. This increases the window of opportunity for insemination.

According to Deb Levine, MA on Webmd.com, there are four stages to the sexual response cycle. "Both men and women go through all four phases, except the timing is different. Men typically reach orgasm first during intercourse, while women may take up to 15 minutes [more] to get to the same place." During the first stage of sex, "Vaginal lubrication begins. The vagina expands and lengthens."[4]

This is a critical fact.

While the vagina has the capacity to expand wide enough to give birth, it's not just a "hole" hanging out there. It's a potential space. If intercourse is attempted without enough foreplay, there will be neither enough space nor enough (natural) lubricant. You can't just add lubricant and overcome this because, enough lubricant or not, the space just isn't there. And that can hurt.

You can't get a cannonball through the barrel of a revolver by adding lubricant.

Compounding this problem is that most women are multi-orgasmic whereas most men are not.

Females can "ejaculate." According to medicalnewstoday. com, "Female ejaculation refers to the expulsion of fluid from a female's urethra during orgasm or sexual arousal."[5] While it may come from the urethra, it's not urine. In chemical properties, it resembles semen. Whatever function this might serve, it doesn't

---

4 https://www.webmd.com/sex-relationships/features/sexual-response-cycle
5 https://www.medicalnewstoday.com/articles/323953

play a critical role in conception. If it did, all females would produce and expel it.

However, when a male ejaculates, from a strictly biological perspective, the sperm in his semen have to travel the entire length of the vagina and into the uterus to fertilize an egg in the Fallopian tube.

Sperm aren't very big. That's a pretty long distance for one to swim. We think it makes perfect sense that males have one big orgasm to give them a powerful send-off. thus giving them a better shot at "finishing the race".

Sperm can live in a woman's body for up to five days, and they swim at about ten miles per hour. Even so, again using nothing more than common sense, it's just logical that the longer the vagina is expanded, the better chance any one sperm is going to have. A sperm count of fifteen million per milliliter or more is considered normal. So, you have a very crowded travel lane there. It would make sense that the wider the highway, the faster more of them can travel.

During orgasm, a woman's vagina contracts rhythmically. That probably doesn't hurt the process either. The longer she remains aroused, the more orgasms she has, the better it is for procreation.

Women might have multiple orgasm more frequently than men do, but there's not the need for a fast send-off. For women, all orgasms don't have to be equal. Typically, they will increase in intensity as time progresses.

If your wife seems like her body works like yours does, that she has one big orgasm and then she's done, that's probably not the case. The orgasms leading up to the "finish" might go unnoticed in the moment, but they are likely still occurring.

So practically speaking, why do we care?

Logistics.

If your wife does not have one big mind-blowing orgasm, it doesn't mean she didn't have one at all. However, not unlike you, she's probably looking for an experience that closely resembles yours. She probably doesn't just want an orgasm; she wants a climax. But her body isn't built that way.

On a practical level, you probably should try to hold off your own finale until she's had hers. When you're done, you're really done. Your wife, on the other hand, will probably still be good to go until she's had the kind of climax that wears her out. If you can't hold out, make sure you're willing to help her through to the end. It is your job to handle your arousal. Few things can irritate a woman as thoroughly as, "I can't wait" if, for some reason, you're both approaching the moment of orgasm at the same time. While this might be true, it will most likely be perceived as selfish and uncaring unless you can continue when you're finished. It doesn't matter if she agrees. If you're unable to continue intercourse for the entire time she desires intercourse, then that's unfair. You need to learn to control your body. Sure, we all like to get lost in the moment, but not at your lover's expense. We believe most women can accept this if you have the energy to stay in the game until she finishes. But make sure you do. If once you orgasm you're out for the count, be a gentleman and subscribe to the principle of, "Ladies first."

The other problematic thing here is the fact that many women can't achieve orgasm through intercourse alone.

According to M J Sherfey:

> Because all embryos, male and female, start life by developing a combined clitoral-penile tubercle....Geneticists have discovered that all human embryos start life as females....About the 2nd month the fetal tests elaborate enough androgens to offset the maternal estrogens and maleness develops. The discussion of clitoral vs. vaginal orgasm is meaningless because orgasm is the result of muscular stretching and fluid produced by the veins filling the fatty tissues. The process is exactly the same in males and females.[6]

When we're talking about woman's erogenous zones, there are two main ones located in the genitals. The G-Spot and the clitoris.

The vagina itself has relatively few nerves which is thought to help women cope with the pain of childbirth. Since there aren't

---

6 https://pubmed.ncbi.nlm.nih.gov/4470128/

many nerves, it makes sense that she isn't stimulated to orgasm by intercourse.

The nerves are really focused in the clitoris. Think about it: her clitoris is the same exact part of the body that in the womb became your penis.

Like a penis, the clitoris can become erect. Finding it though can be a problem:

> While many people think that the clitoris is a small spot just above the vaginal opening, it is, in fact, a much larger complex. The part most visible is the glans, which is 16 millimeters in length, on average. This is the part that most people will be familiar with.
>
> The glans is covered by the prepuce, which is a skin formed from the vaginal labia. Some people liken the prepuce to foreskin. Hidden inside the pubic bone is the rest of the clitoris, and the entire complex is similar in shape to the penis, with a total length of between 9 and 11 centimeters.[7]

Not only is it small, it's hidden inside multiple layers. Far from being a "spot," it's a lot like a micro-penis buried, for the most part, inside her body.

The G-Spot is an area located an inch or two inside the vagina on the anterior wall (the "wall" closest to her belly button; up if she's on her back; away from her butt.) There are several theories on all of this, and we encourage you to search for more information.

Essentially, it runs down along the vaginal wall behind the G-Spot. In fact, the G-Spot may just a part of the complex. Many scientists believe a "vaginal orgasm" results from stimulation provided to the clitoris during intercourse by friction that stimulates it. We agree.

What this means is, there is no orgasm for her unless the clitoris is stimulated.

But intercourse doesn't directly stimulate it. If you want to empathize with her, imagine the only sex you could ever have

---

7 https://www.medicalnewstoday.com/amp/articles/319596

would be to have someone stroke you while you're wearing multiple layers of pants. Well, sure, if you're excited enough, that could get you "off", but how does that prospect sound long-term?

Add yet another problem into the mix. Just before orgasm, the clitoris disappears into its hood.

The epicenter of her pleasure is a small nub roughly the size of one to two pencil erasers buried under a "hood" of skin at the point closest to the outside of her body, with the rest even less exposed. The closer she gets to orgasm the more it retreats.

No wonder many women don't have orgasms during intercourse!

Practically speaking, if you want to satisfy your wife, you're going to have to locate the clitoris if you haven't already. Without manually (or electrically) stimulating it, your wife probably won't have a genuine orgasm.

If she's been faking them, try not to feel offended. It might be because she loves you and is trying to spare your feelings. It might also be because sex hasn't been all that much fun, and she wants to get it over with. If that's the case, then you better find it. Fast.

Luckily, it's not too difficult.

First, locate the G-Spot (no, we're not kidding.) You might want to coordinate this with her. Not all women know their own anatomy so, one way or another this should be fun.

Put one to two fingers inside her against the anterior wall of the vagina. (If she's lying on her back, your palm would be facing up.) the G-Spot is about one to two inches inside. In some women it has a smoother texture than the rest of the vagina. Then push up towards her belly button. You should feel something that feels like a tendon. Place your thumb about a half an inch below the top of her opening. Gradually bring your fingers together and you should feel it. In our experiences, we think it feels like an eraser-sized micro-penis. Regardless, this is the closest you can get to feeling the whole thing.

Your penis has a strip of erectile tissue running along the top of the shaft that fills with blood when you get erect. Hers is very similar. So, to "jerk off" your wife, place your thumb and middle finger on either side of the clitoris a little above it (just below the top of the opening about a half an inch below the whole opening) and spread the skin out so the whole "base" above it becomes taut. (This won't hurt her. When she gets excite there should be lots of natural lubricant and it may be slippery.) Then, using your forefinger, in a motion from side to side (not up and down), gently move the skin of the hood across the clitoris. This is not dissimilar to what you probably do to masturbate. While the term "jerk off" comes from the movement of the hand towards and away from the body, most men move the skin along the shaft, not their hand across the skin. If they touch the head at all, it would be lightly and probably infrequent.

You will likely have to reposition your fingers from time to time because not only can it be slippery, remember, the more excited she gets, the more it will try to pull a disappearing act. This technique minimizes that effect.

Try to reposition your fingers as little as possible. Women take longer to orgasm. But they are much more sensitive to a break in the rhythm than men. Just like you can delay orgasm by taking a brief pause, the brief pause required to reposition also delays her. This might drive her crazy, and not in a good way.

For oral sex, just like a woman pleasuring an uncircumcised man, you must draw back the hood and expose the head. Place two fingers in the same place, just above and to the side of the shaft and spread the skin out and up.

During oral sex, try to maintain a steady rhythm regardless of what you do. Maintain awareness of your wife's reactions. Just like the head of your penis is super-sensitive, so too the head of her clitoris. Except, she's got all those nerves concentrated in a much smaller area. Plus, the head of the clitoris is normally not exposed. Uncircumcised men tend to be more sensitive probably because the foreskin protects the nerves from being stimulated by rubbing against fabric etc. which can desensitize them. (It's not enough to make a big difference from what we can tell.) While you want to apply pressure and friction, don't overdo it. Speed and pressure aren't necessarily more important than a steady rhythm and not pausing at a critical time.

When in doubt, ask her. Everyone is different, regardless of gender. The only expert on your wife's body that you're going to find is her.

Broad Strokes

One last word on foreplay. The biggest sexual organ is the skin. Many couples overlook this. Since your wife needs much more time "getting steam up" than you do, lightly caressing her with a feather touch can go a long way. The backs of the knees, the feet, back of the neck, along the ridge of the ears tend to be very sensitive, but almost any area had potential. You could even try stroking her palm.

The longer you delay genital contact in favor of caressing, the closer she will be to orgasm when you finally strip down. Take your time. Pace yourself.

We hope this chapter has lived up to your hopes and expectations. We saved the topic of sex for last because we think it's very important. Respect, love, attentiveness and a willingness to be open to feedback and experimentation (trying new things but not necessarily implying, nor eliminating, anything beyond "plain" sex) are all key to making love. If you're not making love to your wife already, what are you waiting for?

The take-aways from this chapter are:

1. When there are issues surrounding sex, they are typically related to frequency of sexual relations or the quality.

2. If one partner wants more frequent relations than the other and the causes are not related to a physical inability to perform, the couple needs to communicate to resolve those issues.

3. Refusing to be intimate with a spouse on a regular basis for any reason other than a physical disability will hurt them emotionally. If this cannot be resolved, it can end the marriage.

4. If you cannot resolve your differences regarding the frequency of physical intimacy, you can enter into an "open" marriage but this is unlikely to work and has a much higher chance of being catastrophic. Maintaining a platonic marriage is also very risky. Find a mutually agreeable resolution.

5. An affair is **not** a solution, rather, it functions to delay an inevitable break-up which is just wasting more of your time and hers.

6. Sex is "more important" and has less flexibility for compromise because it's a biological imperative. Mental and emotional needs can be adjusted, but biological needs function as an imperative, so one partner may not be able to adjust their requirements no matter how much they want to be able to do so.

7. "Bad" sex is sex that results in one or both partners not achieving satisfaction as a result of the action or inaction of their partner. It is almost always experienced by the woman and caused by the man.

8. Women typically need more time, foreplay, and emotional support to get into "the mood."

9. Emotional foreplay and post-orgasm support are integral to "making love". Without them, your wife may not be satisfied even if she has an orgasm.

10. Women have a G-Spot which is the area on the anterior wall of the vagina about an inch to two inches inside. They also

have a clitoris which originates from the same embryonic material as a penis and works amazingly similar.

11. All female orgasms are thought to be through clitoral stimulation. Because clitoral stimulation can be too indirect, this is the reason most women cannot orgasm during intercourse.

12. For your wife to climax, you will most likely have to directly stimulate the clitoris.

13. Most women are multi-orgasmic and typically experience a number of smaller orgasms that increase in intensity until they experience a climax.

14. Women take much longer to achieve climax than men; to do this they require time and steady clitoral stimulation with few or no pauses.

Conclusion

There is a certain sadness to any ending. Although we will most likely never meet the majority of those who read this book, it still feels like we've gone on a journey together. In some sense, we miss you already.

We can't but hope you have at a minimum enjoyed the book. We also hope you have spent the time you need, whether it's a short period or long period, to digest the information then determine how to apply it to your relationship. This dedication tells us very clearly that you love your wife very much and are dedicated to your marriage. That's not something one can take for granted in modern society, and we feel sure she will appreciate it as much as we do.

This book is purposely very dense. Never let it be said we wasted a reader's time belaboring a point. On the other hand, no reader can take in 100% of what they read. Further, as you grow, your understanding of the material may mature. We hope you will revisit these pages. There are books we've reread many times, always marveling at some new appreciation of a hidden gem previously missed. Not all books survive the test of time well. We hope this will be one of those in your library that occupies a place of honor in your heart.

If only there were a way to guarantee you that if you work hard enough, there will be the happy ending of your dreams.

We do believe in happy endings.

But we also know no one can offer guarantees.

We sincerely believe it's never too late to rescue a relationship. But we also know not everyone would agree with us.

When you and your wife stood at the altar, in front of your friends, family, and God, something brought you to that point. Your hearts were filled with hope and love.

Reach back into that moment. Find those feelings. Share them with your wife. Even if the passage of time has dulled the rosy glint of new love, you still have many things in common that you can use to rebuild the temple of your love. Rekindling a marriage requires a conscious decision to put aside the negative and embrace the positive.

If you are sincere, honest, and willing to work to make your marriage even more beautiful than it was at that time, we have faith that she will work with you. Marriage can be hard work. But like the old saying, you will get out of it what you put into it.

Twelve step programs emphasize faith and look to the Serenity Prayer for guidance. You don't have to be a specific religion, or religious at all, to appreciate this paraphrase:

> God, grant me the serenity to accept
> the things I can't change,
> Courage to change the things that I can change,
> And wisdom, so I can tell the difference.

If you bought this book just to make a good marriage great, we think that's wonderful. But if your marriage is in real trouble and you turned to us, our last words of wisdom to you are these:

You CAN change how you approach your marriage in word, thought, and deed. You must have known this when you bought this book. It is no less true right now. Have courage. Change is never easy, but it is ALWAYS positive, even if it doesn't feel like it at the time.

You CANNOT change what your wife is going to do in your marriage. If she chooses to change any aspect of herself as a reaction to a change in you, that is her choice. Just as if she chooses not to change. You can love her. You can respect her. But you can't control her. We wish you a state of complete serenity; may you be calm and peaceful as you navigate this change in your relationship, and perhaps your life. For surely, regardless of the ultimate outcome, if you use the information you've learned to change how you relate to your wife, your marriage will change. We sincerely believe and fervently hope this will be a wonderful change that fills you and your wife's lives with love.

148

And if your relationship is truly in jeopardy, then we offer you these last humble words of wisdom. There is only one thing more horrible than having a marriage fall apart. That is, to have a marriage fall apart and to believe in your heart that you could have, should have, done something more. If it is meant to be, you will be her prince again and rescue this relationship. If it is not, know in your heart that you have done your best.

For what it's worth, we believe those who do good things are eventually rewarded. We don't know how, and we're aware that sometimes, in the moment, this may be hard to believe.

We have faith in you. We want to thank you sincerely for choosing to take this journey with us. And we're proud to have you for our student.

God bless you.

Norman Anayeland
March 4, 2020

Acknowledgments

Even without multiple authors writing, there are always plenty of people to thank. We would like to honor the following people without whom this book would not be in your hands, or if it were, it wouldn't be nearly as good.

With our most sincere thanks to Cynthia Anne Bowen, Julius St. Clair, Mark E. Tetreault, Joe D'Silva, Christin Silva-Farrell, and Shadow P. Farrell for all their help.

Bibliography

Barrell, Amanda. "What is female ejaculation?" MedicalNewsToday, 2020, www.medicalnewstoday.com/articles/323953. Accessed 4 March 2020.

Hewings-Martin, Yella. "The ins and outs of the vagina." MedicalNewsToday, 29 September 2020, www.medicalnewstoday.com/amp/articles/319596. Accessed 4 March 2020.

Levine, Deb. "The Sexual-Response Cycle: What Happens to Our Bodies During Sex." WebMD, 1999, www.webmd.com/sex-relationships/features/sexual-response-cycle. Accessed 4 March 2020.

Sherfey M. J. (1974). Some biology of sexuality. Journal of sex & marital therapy, 1(2), 97–109. https://doi.org/10.1080/00926237408405278

CPSIA information can be obtained
at www.ICGtesting.com
Printed in the USA
JSHW020119270420
5313JS00001B/1